Deerfield Academy

THE CAMPUS GUIDE

Deerfield Academy

AN ARCHITECTURAL TOUR BY

Aaron M. Helfand

PHOTOGRAPHS BY ROBERT S. BARNETT

FOREWORD BY JOHN P. N. AUSTIN
ESSAY BY MARGARITA O'BYRNE CURTIS

PRINCETON ARCHITECTURAL PRESS
NEW YORK

Published by
Princeton Architectural Press
202 Warren Street, Hudson, NY 12534
Visit our website at www.papress.com

Printed in China
23 22 21 20 4 3 2 1 First edition

ISBN 978-1-61689-825-0

Program Director, The Campus Guides: Jan Cigliano Hartman
Editor: Linda Lee
Designer: Natalie Snodgrass
Map Art Direction: George Knight
Map Artist: Constance Brown

Library of Congress Cataloging-in-Publication Data
available upon request.

Table of Contents

9 **How to Use This Guide**
10 **Foreword** *by John P. N. Austin*
12 **Tradition and Translation**
by Margarita O'Byrne Curtis

15 **Introduction**

WALK ONE
24 **A Revolution in Learning: Academic Buildings**

WALK TWO
64 **Beyond the Classroom: Buildings for the Arts, Athletics, and Communal Living**

WALK THREE
102 **Finding Home: the Development of the Modern Dormitory**

WALK FOUR
144 **An Extraordinary Legacy: Notable Deerfield Residents and Their Houses**

WALK FIVE
166 **Deerfield and the Broader Community**

202 **Acknowledgments**
205 **Glossary**
212 **Bibliography**
213 **Image Credits**
214 **Index**

How to Use This Guide

This guide is intended for visitors, alumni, students, and faculty who wish to know more about the historically and architecturally significant buildings of Deerfield Academy's campus and its surroundings.

The book is divided into five walks, with buildings grouped thematically. Walks One through Three cover the academic buildings, arts and athletics facilities, and dormitories, respectively. Walks Four and Five include a selection of important houses and other landmarks on campus and in the town of Deerfield. The Introduction provides an overview of the school's historical and geographical context.

Note that Deerfield Academy is a private secondary school, and with the exception of the von Auersperg Gallery and the Academy bookstore in Hitchcock House, Academy buildings are not generally open to the public. Please respect the privacy and safety of the students and faculty, many of whom live on campus. Visitors should not enter any campus building without permission.

Many of the buildings in the town of Deerfield, however, are open to the public. These include a dozen museum houses owned by Historic Deerfield as well as the Memorial Hall Museum, run by the Pocumtuck Valley Memorial Association.

Further Information:

Deerfield Academy
Communications Office
Koch Center, Room 211
PO Box 87
Deerfield, MA 01342
(413) 774-1860
communications@deerfield.edu

von Auersperg Gallery
Hess Center for the Arts
PO Box 87
Deerfield, MA 01342
(413) 774-1480

Historic Deerfield, Inc.
PO Box 321
84B Old Main Street
Deerfield, MA 01342
(413) 774-5581
historic-deerfield.org

Memorial Hall Museum
and PVMA Library
Pocumtuck Valley
Memorial Association
10 Memorial St.
Deerfield, MA 01342
(413) 774-7476
deerfield-ma.org

View of gymnasium from Dining Hall
PREVIOUS **Hitchcock House**

Foreword

I started my Deerfield journey in July of 2019, when I became the Academy's fifty-sixth head of school, and as someone who has long held Deerfield in high esteem, I am honored to contribute to this book.

For new students and their families, and other visitors to campus, Deerfield can be a delight to explore, and I was, likewise, eager to learn more about this exceptional place. I was intrigued by the evolution of a small, local day school to the prestigious, internationally renowned independent school depicted in this guide. What role, I wondered, did buildings and grounds play in this transformation? How did the landscape and a classic New England village help shape Deerfield Academy's values and traditions?

Looking at the Academy's history is an invaluable way to think about its future. How will we—employees, alumni, families, friends, and students—sustain and shape Deerfield by the decisions we make today? And how might our decisions be informed by Deerfield's past?

In asking these questions, I discovered a wonderful facet of this book: the reader can easily access Deerfield—the Academy and the village—in a variety of ways and for a range of purposes. Whether your interest lies in colonial architecture or in the storied history of a remarkable school, this guide is a gift to return to often and savor. By all means, dog-ear your favorite pages, underline salient paragraphs, make notes in the margins, and plan a visit. This kind of low-tech interactivity is as timeless—and relevant—as Deerfield Academy itself and will bring you much joy and knowledge, I am sure.

John P. N. Austin
Head of School
August 2019

John Louis Dormitory

Tradition and Translation

Bruce Barton, a Deerfield parent and trustee, wrote extensively and aptly about the Academy nearly a century ago. In his book *Deerfield Academy* (1929), Barton writes, "There is something about Deerfield that is not easy to put into print—something that you feel in the corridors of its hundred-year-old buildings and the atmosphere of its rugged hills. That something is the New England tradition, the wholesome presence of the New England conscience."

Strolling down Main Street or Albany Road, a visitor to campus will recognize the school Barton described decades ago. Many of our academic and residential buildings recall our history. And nestled between River and Rock—the Deerfield River to the west and the Pocumtuck Ridge to the east—we continue to draw upon our sense of place, our New England roots, to develop character and inculcate in our students the values of hard work, honesty, respect, and concern for others.

We also look outward, beyond our bucolic setting, to strengthen the school. Currently, students hail from more than thirty-five states and as many countries. The Boyden Library—a vibrant academic hub redesigned to meet the challenges of teaching and learning in the twenty-first century—houses the Center for Service and Global Citizenship. The center oversees our travel programs and is the point of departure for those who seek to leave the comforts of campus to gain experience in the wider world.

Deerfield is built on the notion of community, which is central to life here. Whether gathering for all-school meetings in the Large Auditorium—located in the extraordinary Hess Center for the Arts—or rallying our teams on the Lower Level, we come together in support of one another. Throughout our 330-acre campus,

Campus walk looking north

boarding and day students regularly assemble for cocurriculars, to pursue academics, arts, community service, and club activities.

Our sense of community is also expressed through our open campus—you will find very few fences here—and through the bonds that are forged among students and between students and teachers. A distinguishing feature of Deerfield is our residential program. It is a cornerstone of our community. Nearly five hundred and seventy boarding students live in sixteen dormitories alongside faculty residents.

Knowing that our facilities recall our past and support our mission—to inspire students to pursue their passions, becoming the best version of themselves for individual achievement and for the greater good—we have been intentional in modifying Deerfield's built landscape. Step into the Koch Center for Science, Mathematics and Technology; the Athletics Complex; or the Hess Center, and you will discover state-of-the-art spaces that foster imagination, leadership, collaboration, critical thinking, and creativity.

As you delve into Deerfield—via the pages that follow or by visiting campus—you will see that we have preserved our traditions by translating them for the exigencies of our time. You will find a school that remains rooted in its heritage while continually adapting to the modern world.

I hope you enjoy this guide and the story that it tells of this special place.

Margarita O'Byrne Curtis
Head of School, 2006–2019
May 2019

Asa Stebbins House, Historic Deerfield

View from Pocumtuck Ridge

Introduction

The best vantage point from which to see Deerfield Academy in context is known to students as the Rock—a bare sandstone outcropping at the crest of the Pocumtuck Ridge, just east of campus. Edward Hitchcock, headmaster of the Academy from 1816 to 1818, described the view in his monumental *Report on the Geology, Mineralogy, Botany, and Zoology of Massachusetts*, published in 1833:

> Standing...on the western edge of the mountain, a most enchanting panorama opens to view. The alluvial plain on which Deerfield stands is sunk nearly 100 feet below the general level of the Connecticut valley; and at the south-west part of this basin, Deerfield river is seen emerging from the mountains, and winding in the most graceful curves along its whole western border. Still more beneath the eye is the village, remarkable for regularity, and for the number and size of the trees along the principal street. The meadows, a little beyond, are one of the most verdant and fertile spots in New England. Upon the whole, this view is one of the most perfect pictures of rural peace and happiness that can be imagined.

Today, that magnificent view is little changed. Pocumtuck Ridge runs roughly north-south, dividing the glacier-carved valleys of the Deerfield and Connecticut Rivers just to the south of the point where the two rivers merge. During the seventeenth century, as English settlers began to colonize the New England coast, the Connecticut River drew them up, as if by capillary action, from Long Island Sound into the heart of western Massachusetts. Not only was the river easily navigable, its broad floodplain offered farmland of unsurpassed fertility. A series of English towns

View from Pocumtuck Ridge, ca. 1870

quickly sprouted along the river's banks, each one pushing the frontier farther north, from Springfield in 1636 to Northampton in 1654, Hadley in 1659, Hatfield in 1661, and then Deerfield in 1671.

The English, of course, were not the first to settle the so-called Pioneer Valley. For thousands of years, Native American tribes had prized the river and its rich soil. The site that would become the town of Deerfield was home to the Pocumtucks, who were related culturally and linguistically to the Algonquins. The Pocumtucks were seminomadic, moving throughout what is now western Massachusetts, northern Connecticut, and southern Vermont. They settled seasonally to plant cornfields on Deerfield's floodplain until a raid by rival Mohawks destroyed their village in 1664, clearing the way for the colonial settlers.

English towns along the Connecticut were equally vulnerable to attacks by the French in Canada and their Native American allies until the mid-eighteenth century, by which time the frontier had moved farther north and west. Indeed, a Native American attack wiped out the first English settlement at Deerfield (then still known as Pocumtuck) in 1675. The rebuilt town was sacked again by combined French and Indian forces in 1704. (See Walk Five, pages 169 and 174.)

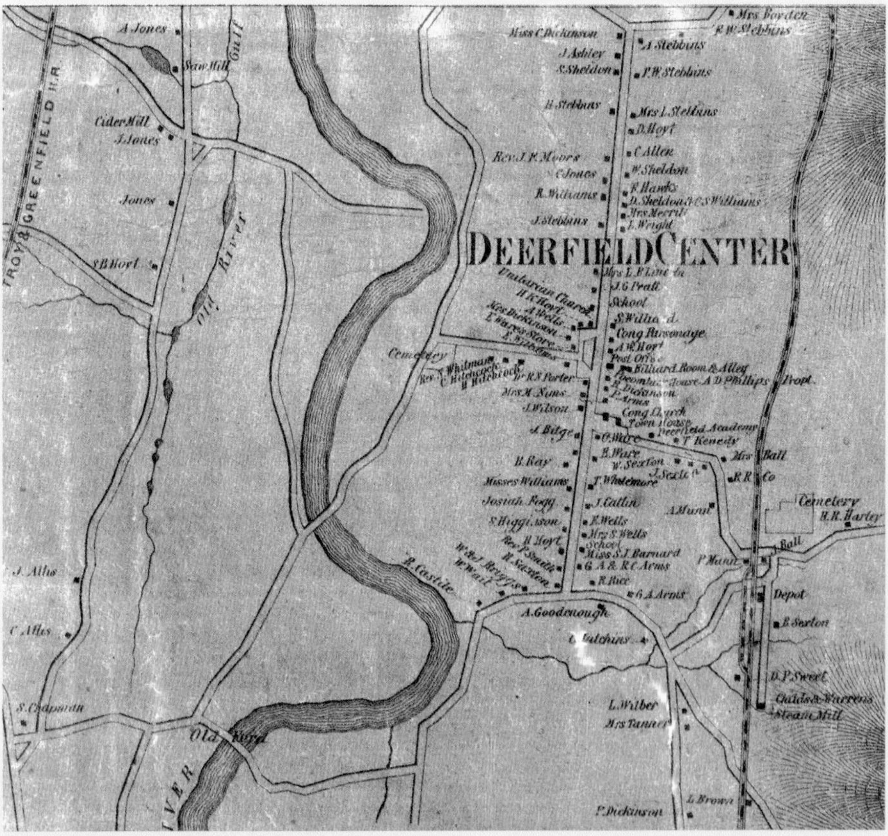

Plan of the Town of Deerfield, 1858

Thereafter, Deerfield was able to rebuild in relative peace, setting the stage for significant growth during the course of the eighteenth century. The town's physical development during this period essentially followed the plan laid out by the first settlers in 1671, and that plan remains virtually unchanged today. The layout takes advantage of a broad plateau that projects westward from the base of the Pocumtuck Ridge toward the Deerfield River such that it slopes steeply downward toward the river's floodplain on the north, west, and south. The village is arrayed along a single mile-long thoroughfare, Old Main Street, known locally as the Street, which runs the length of this plateau from north to south. House lots line up along the Street in a series of long narrow strips extending east and west from either side, with each lot corresponding to additional tracts of farmland in the floodplain below. At the midpoint of the Street, a small parcel of land is set aside as the Town Common, with the Congregational church at its northern edge. By the mid-eighteenth century, the town had established a secondary street, now known as Albany Road, running west from the Common to a ford across the river. A little farther south, another road, now Memorial Street, branched off to the east toward the ridge.

Farm fields along the Deerfield River

View of the Street looking north, ca. 1900; photograph by Frances and Mary Allen

By the end of the eighteenth century, Deerfield's citizens had lined the street with handsome wood-frame houses, each supported by a collection of barns and outbuildings behind. They planted the fields with corn and other crops and raised cattle for sale in Boston. The town had now grown prosperous enough that it could begin to turn at least some of its attention to other endeavors, such as the education of its children. Thus, in the winter of 1797, a group of nineteen prominent citizens from Deerfield and nearby communities gathered at the Barnard Tavern to discuss the creation of a school, and on March 1 of that year, Massachusetts governor Samuel Adams signed a bill granting a charter to found an academy in Deerfield.

This school, which opened with approximately seventy students, has now grown to a student body of 650, and its campus has likewise expanded. Originally contained within a single building, the Academy now occupies more than thirty buildings spread across 330 acres extending on either side of the Street and centered on the Town Common.

In contrast to the secluded character of many preparatory schools (such as St. Paul's or Hotchkiss), Deerfield Academy has always been intimately connected with the town. In the early years, its boarding students lived with local families. During the nineteenth century, the Academy merged for a period of time with the local public school and shared a building with the town library, while its own original building became a museum of local history, the Pocumtuck Valley Memorial Association. In the twentieth century, as the Academy rose to prominence as one of the most prestigious boarding schools in the United States, its presence gave renewed vitality to the town—a welcome boost in an age when small-scale agriculture was no longer enough to sustain a community.

This connection between Deerfield Academy and the village is legible in the architecture of both. As the Academy has grown, almost every architect who contributed to its campus made explicit reference to the features of the colonial village. This trend began in 1798, with the Academy's very first building, but it was legendary headmaster Frank L. Boyden who had the biggest hand in shaping the school's campus. Boyden, who led the school from 1902 until his retirement in 1968, ensured that the school's architecture paid homage to the town's history at the same time that it announced the school's status as a modern educational institution.

While the village has shaped the school's architecture, the inverse is also the case. Over the past century, Boyden and many of the school's trustees, parents, and alumni have played crucial roles in preserving and restoring the village's historic buildings. In doing so, they have drawn upon a rich and pioneering tradition of preservation that began in Deerfield in the mid-nineteenth century. Deerfield's residents were uniquely aware of their town's colonial history, and their efforts to preserve it were some of the earliest in the United States. Their movement inspired like-minded individuals to settle in Deerfield, further enriching the town's deep commitment to the stewardship of its architectural and cultural heritage.

As a result, today both the landscape and the village are remarkably well preserved. One can still swim in the frigid river or stroll through the open fields

Deerfield Academy track, with farm fields beyond

Deerfield River

following its banks—although alongside the cow pastures and rows of corn, one now finds acres of Academy playing fields. Traveling the dirt roads that wind through this landscape, one is likely to encounter students or faculty members out for a run, or visitors from out of town who have come to see the village's historic houses. The rocky summit of the Pocumtuck Ridge from which Hitchcock contemplated New England's ancient landscape is still accessible to those up for a brisk hike. The landscape is more wooded now than it was in 1833, but the view is still spectacular.

Likewise, it is still possible to walk along the tree-lined Street and admire the old farmhouses, most of them looking just as they did more than two centuries ago. Only one or two remain connected to a working farm, however. Many are owned by Deerfield Academy, which maintains them as residences for some faculty members. Others have been restored and preserved as museum houses by Historic Deerfield, an institution founded by Deerfield Academy parents Henry and Helen Flynt. These houses are open to the public on a regular basis, drawing tourists from around the world.

Given the unique bond between Academy and town, this book is a guide to both. The primary focus is on the campus itself: Walks One through Three portray the school's academic buildings, extracurricular facilities, and dormitories, respectively. Together, they cover all the buildings on campus as well as several that no longer exist. Walk Four discusses some of the notable people who have lived in the town of Deerfield—many of whom were also connected with the Academy—along with the houses they lived in. Walk Five examines a variety of significant buildings and institutions in both the town and the surrounding region and the impact they have had on the experience of the Academy's students. In these five walks, the guide aims to present a history of this remarkable school and village through the lens of architecture and campus design.

This book is the first to examine all of Deerfield Academy's buildings in detail. There are several other books that deal with the town's residential architecture much more comprehensively. For those seeking additional information on the historic houses, Family & Landscape: Deerfield Homelots from 1671, *by Susan McGowan and Amelia Miller (Pocumtuck Valley Memorial Association, 1996) will be of interest—it details the history of each of the original properties along the Street. Further documentation of the museum houses owned by Historic Deerfield may be found in* Historic Deerfield: A Portrait of Early America, *by Elizabeth Stillinger (Dutton Studio Books, 1992). Other relevant books may be found in the bibliography.*

The Street

WALK ONE

A Revolution in Learning: Academic Buildings

1 Memorial Hall Museum (original Academy Building)
2 Deerfield Academy and Dickinson High School Building *(demolished)*
3 Main School Building
4 Pocumtuck Buttonball Tree
5 Arms Building
6 Kendall Classroom Building
7 Brooke's Garden
8 Frank L. and Helen Childs Boyden Library
9 Longitude Dial
10 Helen Childs Boyden Science Center *(demolished)*
11 Koch Center for Science, Mathematics and Technology

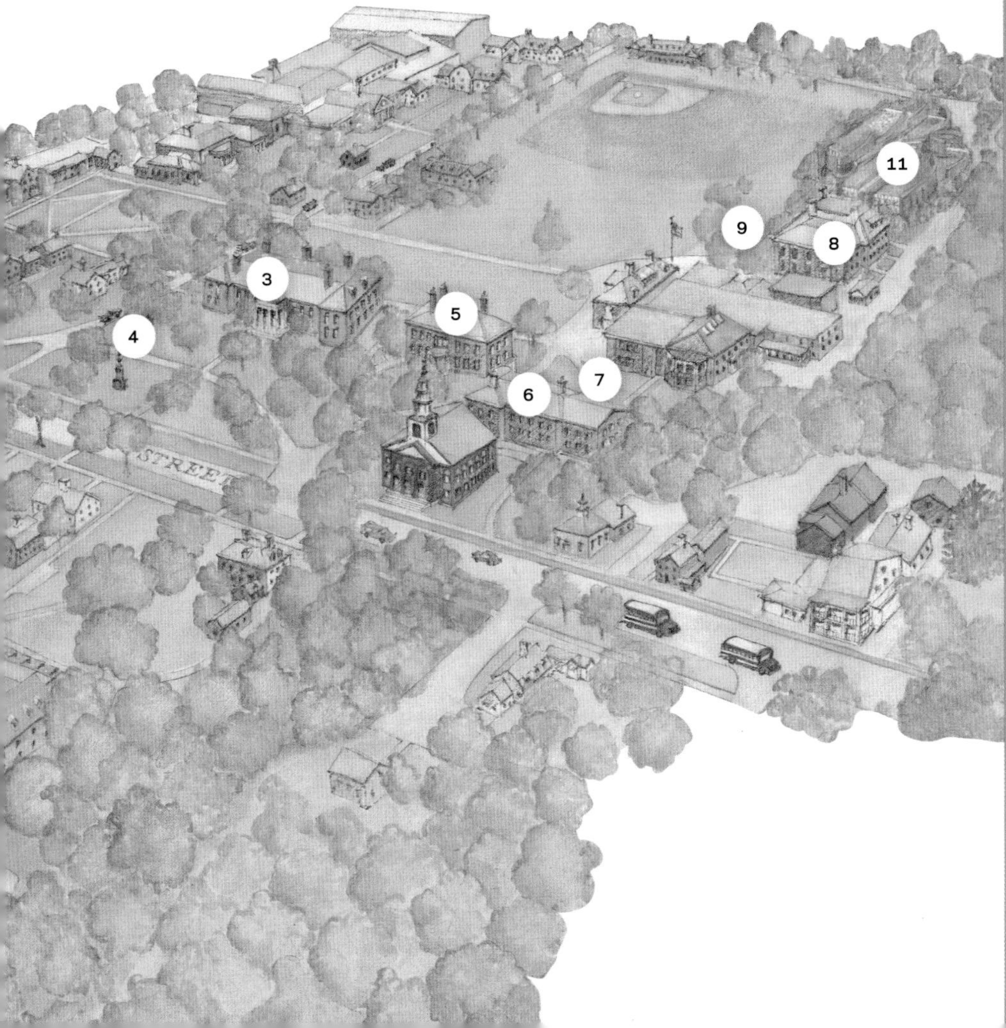
11
9
8
3
5
4
7
6
STREET

WALK ONE

A Revolution in Learning: Academic Buildings

When Deerfield Academy first opened to students in 1799, it occupied a modest footprint consisting of a single building with five rooms. Today, the 330-acre campus includes more than thirty buildings, with a half dozen devoted to classroom space. As the school grew from seventy students to over six hundred, it supplemented its classrooms with lecture halls, seminar rooms, libraries, art and architecture studios, concert halls, science labs, computer labs, and even a planetarium.

The bulk of this expansion has occurred over the past one hundred years. During the whole of the nineteenth century, Deerfield Academy's campus was never larger than a single building: the original Academy Building was used until 1878, when the school moved to a second structure, on the site of the current Main School Building. During the twentieth century, however, the school's academic mission and its campus rapidly expanded. Frank L. Boyden, who served as headmaster from 1902 to 1968, transformed what had become a primarily local institution into the internationally recognized school it is today. Boyden oversaw a dramatic increase in the size of the student body and faculty, as well as a reformation of the curriculum, with a new focus on preparing students for the country's best colleges and universities.

Boyden placed a strong emphasis on improving the Academy's facilities as well. Under his leadership, the campus grew to more than two dozen buildings, such that by the time he retired, the school resembled a small college campus. Almost all of these buildings were designed by a single family of architects: Charles Platt and his sons, William and Geoffrey. Over the course of four decades, Boyden and the Platts unwaveringly pursued their shared architectural vision for the school, giving the campus a remarkably cohesive architectural character and setting the tone for many subsequent projects. As noted in the Introduction, it was a vision that drew heavily from the town's colonial history at the same time that it asserted the Academy as a leading institution of modern learning.

The transformation that Boyden initiated continued under the leadership of subsequent heads of school (David Pynchon, Robert Kaufmann, Eric Widmer, Margarita Curtis, and John Austin). Their most notable additions to the campus have included enlargements to the arts and athletics complexes (discussed in Walk Two, pages 67 and 88) and the construction of two successive science buildings, the first built in 1974 and the second replacing it some thirty years later.

This walk is organized chronologically (a sequence that also happens to coincide with a straightforward geographical path). We begin on Memorial Street, at the Academy's first building, dated 1798, which is now home to the Memorial Hall Museum. We then proceed to the Town Common, the center of Deerfield's current campus, where the Academy built its second schoolhouse in 1878, then replaced it with the current Main School Building in 1930. From here, we walk north, then west,

OPPOSITE **Memorial Hall Museum**

moving counterclockwise around the Academy's main Quad, skipping only the Hess Center for the Arts, which is discussed in Walk Two. We end with the Koch Center for Science, Math and Technology, completed in 2007.

1 Memorial Hall Museum (original Academy Building)

Asher Benjamin, 1798; additions, architect unknown, 1810; architect unknown, 1916; and Richard Butterfield, 1970

In June of 1799, Deerfield Academy's second headmaster, Claudius Herrick, wrote a letter to an acquaintance, urging him to come and teach at the fledgling school. He described the new Academy Building as a particular draw: "The Academy is an elegant Edifice, having, on the lower floor, four rooms, one for the English school, one for the Latin, & Greek school, the Preceptor's room, and a room for the Museum and Library. The upper room, being all in one, is used for examinations, and exhibitions."

Herrick depicted the Academy as being in "a very flourishing state," with two "assistants," or teachers, and more than seventy students attending that quarter. Two-thirds of the students, "the children of Gentlemen," came from neighboring towns and boarded with village families. More than twenty boys studied Latin and Greek and between twenty and thirty girls studied English grammar and geography. "I will assure you, Sir," Herrick wrote, "we have no small number of young gentlemen, and ladies, in the Academy whose society is very agreeable."

Memorial Hall Museum, historic classroom

Deerfield constructed the large brick Academy Building on what is now Memorial Street soon after the school's founding in 1797. It has been expanded and remodeled several times since then, first to accommodate the growth of the Academy and subsequently to house the Pocumtuck Valley Memorial Association (PVMA), which purchased the building when the Academy moved to its current location in 1878.

Today, the building is composed of two similar wings connected in the middle by a recessed hyphen. Viewed from Memorial Street, the left-hand (western) wing is the oldest portion of the building, but its appearance has been much altered over the years. The hyphen dates from 1916. The right-hand (eastern) wing was built in 1970, but its architect, Richard Butterfield, designed it as a near-replica of what the original block had looked like around 1810.

The eminent neoclassical architect Asher Benjamin is responsible for the Academy Building's original design. When he received the commission in 1797, Benjamin was twenty-four years old and living just a few miles north of Deerfield, in Greenfield. He was only beginning his career, and he would go on to design dozens of houses and churches throughout New England. His projects were at first strongly influenced by the Federal-style work of Boston architect Charles Bulfinch, though he later became a leading exponent of the Greek Revival style. In addition to his many built works, he published seven widely distributed pattern books (printed volumes of architectural designs for builders to follow), leading him to become one of the most influential American architects of the early nineteenth century.

As first designed, the Academy Building was a quintessential example of Benjamin's simple yet elegant classical style: a symmetrical brick structure two stories tall and six bays wide, capped by a low hipped roof with a wood cupola. The original facade featured two identical front doors: one for the Latin and Greek school, the other for the English school. Each door was surmounted by semicircular transom windows and set within a brick arch with a series of projecting brick voussoirs. One can accurately visualize this building by imagining the 1970 wing with the third floor omitted.

It is notable that, from the start, the Academy Building included a museum on its ground floor. This space featured local Native American artifacts, along with curiosities from around the world. It is considered one of the earliest museums in the country and was a sign of Deerfield residents' early historical awareness, as well as a precursor to the Memorial Hall Museum that would eventually occupy the space.

A decade later, the thriving school had outgrown Benjamin's original Academy Building and embarked on a major expansion. This project more than doubled the building's size and for the first time allowed the school to provide on-site accommodations for boarding students. The work added a third story to the original block and a three-story wing to the rear. The whole structure was united under a delicately detailed wood cornice, a portion of which is still visible on the back of the building, and the cupola was reconstructed on the new roof.

By 1855, the school had replaced the pair of arched front doors with a single large door on the left and a window on the right. The brick outline of the original right-hand door is visible today, but in the nineteenth century, the whole building was painted white, masking the patched brickwork. Also during this period, the second floor was partitioned into three smaller rooms, with the westernmost room becoming the school library.

Deerfield Academy occupied this enlarged structure until 1878, when it moved to a new building on the Town Common. The original Academy Building was then sold to the recently established PVMA, which undertook major renovation work, transforming the school building into the Memorial Hall Museum, a repository of local history.

This remarkable museum, which still occupies the building today, displays a wide range of artifacts from the town's early history and includes the country's first examples of "period rooms," reconstructions of historic interiors furnished with period-appropriate antiques. One of the most impressive relics in the collection is the "old Indian door," once the front entrance to the 1699 Ensign John Sheldon House. This house was one of few structures in Deerfield to survive the notorious French and Indian raid of 1704, and the door bears dramatic hatchet marks where attackers hacked a hole large enough to shoot a musket through, killing Sheldon's wife, Hannah. (This episode is discussed further in Walk Five, page 174). In 1847, the owner of the Old Indian House, as it had come to be known, decided to tear it down

Memorial Hall Museum, library

and replace it with a new one. Alarmed Deerfield residents, led by a prominent minister and educator, the Reverend Samuel Willard, spearheaded a campaign to save the historic home. Although their efforts failed and the owner demolished the Old Indian House in 1848, the town did recover the front door and several other fragments. This act was one of the earliest recorded preservation efforts in the United States. The participants went on to found the PVMA and are widely regarded as pioneering in their desire to preserve early American history for posterity.

In his 1890 "History of Memorial Hall" (published in the *History and Proceedings of the Pocumtuck Valley Memorial Association*), PVMA president George Sheldon (a descendant of Ensign John Sheldon) describes the original concept for the museum as envisioned by the association's leading members: "The committee thought it well to set apart one room for the display of Indian relics, including of course the 'old Indian door'; another in which to exhibit an old family kitchen; one for an old-time parlor; one for an ancient bed-room; one in which shall be shown all the apparatus for making linen cloth as our grandmothers did it; one for farming utensils of 'ye olden time'; and others as may be deemed necessary." The museum still displays the door and other pieces salvaged from the Old Indian House. A set of large marble tablets installed on the museum's second floor memorializes those Deerfield residents killed during the raid.

Memorial Hall Museum, period room

In addition to commemorating the seventeenth- and eighteenth-century history of the town of Deerfield, the Memorial Hall Museum also preserves many elements of Deerfield Academy's early years, including a fully furnished classroom, the school's own Williams Museum (a small cabinet of curiosities), a number of early nineteenth-century scientific instruments, and the original bell that had hung in the cupola.

Interestingly, in an era when eighteenth-century architecture was only beginning to be appreciated again, the PVMA recognized the historic significance of the Academy Building itself and characterized its renovation explicitly in terms of historic preservation. At the dedication ceremony, George Sheldon declared: "We this day meet to dedicate this grand old building to public use as a Memorial Hall—itself a venerable relic battered and scarred by the assaults of four score years, and many generations of boys, which, when it fell into the hands of the association, was fast returning to the elements. Decay has now been arrested—its youth renewed. It stands to-day as firm as the hills, securely infolding [*sic*] within its ample bosom our gathered treasures."

The PVMA's pioneering efforts at architectural preservation would have a lasting effect on the village of Deerfield, setting the course for the restoration of many buildings and the preservation of the town's colonial history. These efforts would ultimately also shape the direction of Deerfield Academy's campus design.

Old Indian House door

Nonetheless, the PVMA's renovation of the Academy Building was a pragmatic blend of restoration and modernization: the association installed a fireproof brick wall between the original block and the 1810 wing, removed partitions in the third floor, and raised the exterior walls by three feet to allow for a large exhibition hall. On the exterior, the additional three feet were occupied by a characteristically Victorian brick cornice, completely out of character with the style of the rest of the building. To help support this additional masonry, the flat arches of the third-floor windows were rebuilt as segmental arches. The renovation also included modifications to the front door, a coat of red paint to the exterior, and a new metal roof. Unfortunately, the cupola, which had been removed sometime between 1855 and 1879, was not reconstructed.

The PVMA expanded Memorial Hall in 1916 thanks to a donation by George and Jennie Arms Sheldon. (For more on Jennie Sheldon, see Walk Two, page 72; for more on George Sheldon, see Walk Four, page 161). The three-story addition to the northeast matched the architectural style of the rest of the building (in its post-1880 form) but used modern fireproof construction for safe storage of the museum's library of books, pamphlets, maps, and paintings. It sits back from the main facade, in deference to the original building.

The association completed its most recent addition in 1970; the new east wing housing the combined libraries of the PVMA and Historic Deerfield. The exterior of this wing accurately replicates the design of the original building prior to its Victorian alterations, and it helpfully steps forward to stand side by side with the original, inviting us to compare the two. Additional restoration work completed during the same building campaign included the complete dismantling and reconstruction of the 1810 wing, which had become structurally unstable.

The Memorial Hall Museum is open to the public from May through October; its impressive collections include several exhibits of historic artifacts that remain as they were originally conceived in 1878.

2 Deerfield Academy and Dickinson High School Building

Peabody & Stearns, 1878; demolished, 1930

In 1858, the town of Deerfield was indicted for violating an 1827 Massachusetts law that required any town with more than five hundred residents to provide free public secondary education. Working with town leaders, the trustees of Deerfield Academy agreed to create a free high school component, with costs shared between the town and the Academy. This arrangement continued until 1875, when the town received a transformational bequest from longtime resident Esther Dickinson.

Esther had married Consider "Uncle Sid" Dickinson, a Revolutionary War veteran who, at age eighty, was thirty years her senior. Uncle Sid was notoriously frugal; town lore claims he married Esther, his second wife, because he said it was cheaper to support a wife than hire a housekeeper. Unsurprisingly, the two bore no children. They agreed that they would use their estate—which was substantial because of Consider's "industry, good judgment and economy"—to fund the education of Deerfield residents. Accordingly, Esther's will bequeathed her property and $50,000 for the construction and endowment of a public high school and a town library.

Deerfield Academy then proposed that a joint institution, the "Deerfield Academy and Dickinson High School," be housed in the new building, which was to be constructed on the Town Common at the site of Dickinson's home. To make way for the new structure, her own house was moved to its current site along Albany Road. This house, originally built by Elijah Williams in 1760, was also given to the Academy and would become the school's first dedicated dormitory in 1916. (See Walk Three, page 109.)

The new school building was completed in 1878. An 1880 prospectus describes it as "an artistic brick structure…the best equipped school building in the vicinity, having: Two large school rooms, well-appointed physical and chemical laboratories, a music room, a natural history room, and a capacious hall furnished to accommodate between three and four hundred persons, devoted to the use of the school. In addition, the building contains a public reading room and library, which furnish valuable works of reference."

Forty-one boys and thirty-six girls attended the Deerfield Academy and Dickinson High School when the school opened its doors in 1878. Students from the town of Deerfield attended the new school free of charge, thanks to the generous endowment Dickinson had provided, while other students paid a modest tuition. All students had to pass an entrance exam to be admitted. At the time, the school's faculty consisted of a principal and only four other instructors, yet—in part thanks to its modern new building—the school was able to offer a broad course of study, including classical and modern languages, English and American literature, rhetoric, history, political economy, civil government, business arithmetic, algebra, geometry, physics, chemistry, geology, botany, zoology, physiology, drawing, and music.

The architect of the new building was the Boston firm of Peabody & Stearns, which was active from 1870 to 1917 and was one of the most distinguished firms in the country. Though still young in 1877, the office had already completed numerous prestigious commissions, including Matthews Hall at Harvard University, College Hall at Smith College, and several large houses in Boston and Newport.

For most of their early projects, the architects had worked in some variant of the Victorian Gothic style, but at Deerfield they tried something new: a picturesque Anglo-American classicism known as the Queen Anne style. Pioneered in England by Richard Norman Shaw, this style drew its forms from seventeenth- and eighteenth-century sources but reassembled them into whimsical and delicately ornamented compositions. American architects, led by Robert Peabody, were quick to develop their own parallel version, which drew primarily from colonial sources—that is, from precisely the kinds of buildings that defined the town of Deerfield. During the same year the Dickinson High School Building was in design, Peabody published several articles in *American Architect and Building News* in which he argued for the

Dickinson High School Building

Queen Anne style as a natural extension of American colonial architecture, especially appropriate in New England. Indeed, the style can be accurately understood as the first phase of the Colonial Revival, which would become one of the most popular American architectural styles of the twentieth century, dominating many academic campuses, including Deerfield's.

In April of 1878, *American Architect and Building News* published an illustration of the school building alongside a reconstructed rendering of the demolished 1699 Ensign John Sheldon House, underscoring its colonial inspiration. Likewise, an article in *The Greenfield Gazette and Courier* from December 1878 observed that the Dickinson High School's position at the center of the historic village "suggested the design of an old-fashioned character; and while the plan is well adapted to school and library purposes, the small-paned sashes, the classical wooden cornices, the door pediment, the belfry, the elliptical arches, recall colonial work and bring the building into harmony with the old mansions and trees of the town....The building is odd and quaint, but, on the whole, very satisfactory, and a great ornament to the village."

Despite its claim to being one of the first Colonial Revival buildings in the United States, its playfully eccentric composition was a far cry from the staid simplicity of Deerfield's eighteenth-century structures. The main facade was dominated by a large mass on the south side, housing the classrooms and lecture hall, and a smaller wing on the north, housing the town library and public reading room. Between these two wings were science labs as well as an entry and stair hall, marked by an ornate tower. The two wings and the tower had steeply pitched front-facing gables, creating the impression of a collection of smaller buildings. Each gable was given its own distinct architectural character, but they shared the same roof pitch and all used a similar vocabulary of classical architectural forms, loosely derived from the English Georgian and American Colonial, and reinterpreted with delicacy and whimsy.

Sadly, this charming and historically important early work of Peabody & Stearns was not to last. Fifty years after its construction, the Colonial Revival movement had evolved to a point where the eccentric early examples had become highly unfashionable—seeming, by then, more Victorian than Colonial—and the school tore down the building to make way for a new Main School Building, designed in an equally beautiful but more sober brand of classicism.

3 Main School Building

Charles A. Platt, 1931; addition, William & Geoffrey Platt, 1958; third-floor renovation, Kuhn Riddle Architects, 2006

Today, the heart of Deerfield Academy's campus is the Main School Building. This stately brick structure presides over the Town Common, rivaled in prominence only by the Brick Church. Its construction marks the beginning of a significant chapter in the history of the school.

During the thirty years leading up to the construction of the Main School Building, Frank L. Boyden held the post of headmaster at the Deerfield Academy and Dickinson High School. When he first arrived at the school in August of 1902, Boyden had just graduated from Amherst College and was seeking a temporary job in order to save up money for law school. Many of the Academy's trustees also expected the job would not last long; at that point, the school had fallen into such a state of neglect that only fourteen students remained. As one of the trustees told Boyden, they considered it "a tossup whether the school [needed] a new headmaster or an undertaker."

Boyden remained in his "temporary" post for sixty-six years. During this time, he transformed the tiny provincial school he had inherited into a nationally renowned academic powerhouse. Already, by the late 1920s, the number of students and faculty had increased—227 students attended during the 1929–30 academic year—and the school's reputation had grown; the physical campus, however, remained underwhelming in comparison with many other boarding schools. It consisted of the Dickinson High School building (rather dilapidated by that point), two wood-frame dormitories, and a handful of old, repurposed houses and barns. Boyden had overseen construction of several new buildings, but so far, his ambitions had been modest. He had built an enviable reputation for the school; he now needed architecture of equal caliber.

Olmsted Brothers model, showing the campus ca. 1929

Boyden mulled over a variety of plans for several years before he could start work on the new academic building. Whereas less than a decade earlier he was hiring local architects in Greenfield, now Boyden was able to consider the country's top firms as candidates to develop the campus. Several offices submitted proposals, but by 1928, Boyden was most interested in the Boston firm of Perry, Shaw & Hepburn. This office was at the time beginning work on the massive restoration and reconstruction of Colonial Williamsburg, a fact that suggests that Boyden had already determined that Deerfield's colonial architecture would provide the stylistic touchstone for his new buildings.

Correspondence from the period indicates that Perry, Shaw & Hepburn developed detailed plans between 1928 and 1929 for several major buildings that would make up the new core of the campus. These included a classroom building, a science building, and a dormitory. However, none of the firm's designs were destined to be built.

In 1929, banker and philanthropist Thomas Cochran expressed interest in making a major contribution to Deerfield's building fund. Cochran had no personal connection to Deerfield. He was a graduate of Phillips Academy Andover, and he gave generously to his alma mater. In those days, however, it was not unusual for wealthy philanthropists to support several institutions, and headmasters at peer schools frequently recommended—and on occasion even financially supported—Deerfield. Cochran visited the Academy, met Boyden and several trustees, and came to the opinion that "few secondary schools are as worthy of financial assistance as Deerfield Academy.... It presents, at the moment, the most inspiring opportunity of which I know, for constructive service in the field of secondary education."

OVERLEAF **Main School Building**

Cochran had earlier donated several major buildings to Andover, and one of the principal conditions of his gift to Deerfield was that the school use the same architect: Charles A. Platt (coincidentally, a cousin of Academy trustee Frank Cheney). In no position to argue, Boyden obligingly settled his account with Perry, Shaw & Hepburn and welcomed Platt to Deerfield. It proved to be a good match: Platt and his sons would go on to design at least eighteen buildings for Deerfield over the course of the next four decades, providing the campus with a remarkably unified architectural identity.

Even were it not for Cochran's insistence, Boyden would have been inclined to appreciate Platt's approach to architecture. Platt was best known for his elegant country houses, often taking inspiration from eighteenth-century American and English precedents. This approach carried over into his institutional work at Andover, where his projects included the Oliver Wendell Holmes Library, the Cochran Chapel, and the Addison Gallery, among others.

His design for Deerfield's Main School Building is very much in the same vein as his work at Andover. Stylistically, it belongs solidly to the Colonial Revival, drawing inspiration from eighteenth-century architecture and disregarding more recent nineteenth-century stylistic developments, such as those incorporated into Peabody & Stearns's design for the 1878 school building. As if to underscore this fact, the 1878 school building was demolished in 1930 to make way for Platt's building. Whereas Peabody & Stearns had been freewheeling and playful in their interpretation of colonial style, Platt adopted an orderly, symmetrical composition, more in tune with the classical and Palladian sources of eighteenth-century American architecture.

Though more faithful to colonial precedent than the building it replaced, Platt's design is no historical replica. Compared with an actual eighteenth-century American building, like Deerfield's own original Academy Building, the architecture of the Main School Building is far more ambitious, in both scale and detailing. Indeed, it is perhaps more closely related to English Georgian and Carolean country houses than to any American colonial buildings. Compare it, for example, with Belton House: this English country house, completed in 1688, appears to have provided the inspiration for the overall composition as well as some of the details, such as the prominent chimneys with their jaunty chimney pots (a feature rarely seen in New England).

Although only two and a half stories tall, the Main School Building feels grander than the three-story original Academy Building because of the larger scale of its features, such as doors, windows, and chimneys. Consider the windows, for example: in the original Academy Building, the windows were the same size as those of a typical house from the same period; by contrast, windows in the Main School Building are twice as large. Similarly, the Main School Building's entrance is not just a simple residential-scale door but three sets of large double doors with transom windows gathered together under a monumental two-story classical Ionic portico. Whereas the old Academy Building was a simple box, the massing of the Main School

OPPOSITE **Main School Building, lobby**

Building is enriched by its projecting portico and wings, creating a five-part facade. Finally, instead of wood trim, Platt employs handsomely carved Indiana limestone.

The interior is similarly lavish. A broad, central hallway runs the length of the building on both floors, opening onto offices on the ground floor and classrooms on the second floor. The entrance lobby is conceived as an elegant yet inviting living room, with a layout similar to the common rooms designed for Boyden and Plunkett Halls, two dormitories built in the 1920s. The lobby's focal point is a large fireplace, which is used on a regular basis during the winter—especially on Friday afternoons when students gather in the lobby to enjoy cookies and hot cocoa.

The design of this lobby was of particular importance to Boyden. In the old school building, he had set up a card table and did his work next to a radiator just inside the front door—not because he did not have an office but because he liked to keep an eye on his school and his students. In the new building, Boyden asked that Platt design a wide, central space just opposite the front door where foot traffic was heaviest. He placed his desk there and, from this perch, kept watch over the school, even as he dictated letters, took phone calls, and held appointments. In *The Headmaster*, John McPhee (class of 1949) describes how Boyden had "a remarkable eye for trouble," and if he sensed a boy was having a hard time, he would pull him aside as he walked to class. Under the pretext of having some quick question, he would try to get to the heart of his student's problem and provide counsel. Boyden continued to work—and watch—from the Main School Building lobby until his retirement, and his desk still remains in this spot.

Main School Building, Caswell Library

The architectural highlight of the Main School Building's interior is the Caswell Library, which occupies the ground floor of the south wing. Entered from the main hallway through a pair of French doors with an elliptical transom, this room is similar in style to the reading room of Platt's Holmes Library at Andover, with stained oak paneling and a plaster ceiling. It features two fireplaces with black marble surrounds, above which hang large portraits of Frank and Helen Boyden framed by exquisitely carved oak garlands. This is the finest room in the entire campus, and it remains in pristine condition.

4 Pocumtuck Buttonball Tree

Directly in front of the Main School Building stands one of the most remarkable trees in New England. It is an American sycamore (*Platanus occidentalis*), also known as a buttonball from its spherical seed clusters. The tree is estimated to be between 350 and 400 years old, likely predating European settlement of Deerfield. It reaches well over one hundred feet in height, and the circumference of its trunk is just over twenty-two feet. There are several other enormous sycamores in the area, with the largest to be found just across the Connecticut River from Deerfield, in Sunderland.

Pocumtuck buttonball tree

5 Arms Building

Charles A. Platt (with William & Geoffrey Platt), 1933

The second major academic building that Charles Platt designed for Deerfield was the Arms Building, which originally housed science labs and is now used as humanities classrooms. Construction was funded by a $100,000 gift from Jennie Maria Arms Sheldon, an MIT-educated scientist and Academy trustee. (See Walk Two, page 72.) Sheldon dedicated the building to the memory of her father, George Albert Arms, whom she described as "a mechanical man who believed in the kind of

Arms Building

education that would make every boy and girl self-supporting." The building included classrooms and well-equipped teaching labs, which were complete with chemical fume hoods (attractively encased in paneled oak) and rows of lab benches supplied with water and gas lines.

Though he equipped it with the most up-to-date technology of the time, Platt designed the Arms Building to be in complete harmony with its historic architectural setting. Standing side by side with the Main School Building on the Town Common, it follows a similar style: brick Georgian/Colonial Revival with eight-over-twelve-pane double-hung windows and a hipped slate roof marked by prominent chimneys. Yet it is somewhat smaller, and every detail is slightly scaled down, carefully calibrated so as not to upstage the Main School Building. Platt even took the chimneys into account, with four chimney pots apiece instead of five.

The focal point of the facade is the entrance portico, again scaled down from the grand, two-story Ionic version found on the Main School Building to a more intimate, semicircular, one-story porch following a modified Doric order. Within the porch, the brick facade is coated with a layer of stucco, and the pair of entrance doors, with their transom window and integrated lantern, is set within a paneled wood surround. Above the portico, a three-part window admits light into the central stair hall and is flanked by a pair of decorative roundels. The portico was originally crowned by a graceful parapet, now missing.

In contrast to its subtle exterior, the interior of the Arms Building is surprisingly dynamic. On entering, one passes through a small vestibule into a dramatically vertical stair hall lit from the large windows above; on turning around, one discovers that the vestibule is tucked underneath the landing of the stair as it doubles back over the entrance.

The second-floor hall is supported by a pair of columns, which also serve to frame the entrance to the first-floor faculty lounge directly across from the main entrance. The columns themselves are remarkable. They are loosely based on the classical Corinthian order, but instead of the traditional acanthus leaves, their capitals are composed of ears of corn and wheat. This detail is a variant of similar corncob capitals designed by Benjamin Latrobe for the US Capitol in the early nineteenth century. It is an emblem of American innovation within the classical tradition and one particularly apt on a campus surrounded by cornfields.

Passing between the columns, one arrives at the faculty lounge (originally the Science Library), which is similar in style to the larger Caswell Library in the Main School Building. This oak-paneled room is organized around a marble fireplace, above which hangs a portrait of Sheldon. Three large double-hung windows look west onto the Quad, while the opposite wall is lined with built-in cabinets and bookcases.

Platt died the same year that the Arms Building opened, only four years after beginning his work at Deerfield and having completed only the Main School Building, the Arms Building, and the Gymnasium. With just these three buildings, though, he dramatically raised the school's standard of architecture and established a long-term vision for an expansive, coherently planned, and stylistically harmonious

Arms Building, interior capital detail

Arms Building, faculty lounge

campus. This vision, eventually carried out by his sons William and Geoffrey, would come to define the campus more than that of any other architect in the entire 220-year history of the school. Platt's finely tuned Colonial Revival designs deftly rooted the Academy in local traditions while at the same time distinguishing it as a world-class institution of learning.

6 Kendall Classroom Building

William & Geoffrey Platt, 1960

During the last years of Charles Platt's career, his sons, William and Geoffrey, assisted him in the office. After Charles's death in 1933, the brothers took over their father's practice and continued as the primary architects of the Deerfield campus.

Kendall Classroom Building

The Platt sons remained faithful to their father's stylistic vision for a distinguished Colonial Revival campus, and their work from 1933 until 1968 represents a remarkable aesthetic continuity with the three buildings Charles designed: the Main School Building, Arms Building, and Gymnasium. This is especially notable given the changes in architectural fashion seen elsewhere during those decades.

By the time William and Geoffrey designed the Kendall Classroom Building in 1960, they had already completed the Dining Hall, Infirmary, Memorial Building, and West Gym as well as a number of dormitories. The Kendall Classroom Building maintains the same brick Georgian/Colonial Revival idiom as the Main School Building and Arms Building. It occupies a prominent location between the Brick Church and the Arms Building, facing onto the Town Common. The principal facade is perpendicular to that of the Arms Building, but in contrast to the earlier building, the Kendall Classroom Building is narrower and its ceiling heights are less generous, resulting in a lower profile. Both buildings, however, feature similar windows and simple hipped roofs punctuated by large chimneys. In addition, each has a one-story classical entrance portico of a simplified Doric order. As with the Arms Building, the facade within the portico is clad with a contrasting material—here horizontal wood boards—to set it apart from the rest of the facade.

Inside, the wood-paneled main lobby and stair hall spans the width of the building. A column screen, reminiscent of the Arms Building but less inventive and without the same sense of spatial drama, demarcates the stairs. Beyond the lobby, the architecture is utilitarian: each floor consists of a single corridor running the length of the building with a series of classrooms opening off each side. A small auditorium occupies the rear of the building on the ground level.

7 Brooke's Garden

To the north of the Arms Building is a small quadrangle, bounded on the east by the Kendall Classroom Building and to the west by the Hess Center for the Arts. In 1998, the Academy relandscaped the southeastern portion of this quadrangle as a garden in memory of Brooke Gonzalez (class of 1997). Gonzalez was vice president of her senior class and was twice a member of the US International 420 Sailing Team. She died in an automobile accident during her first year at Brown University. The centerpiece of the garden is a circular terrace paved in cobblestones and framed on the east by a curved stone bench. The bench is inscribed with the names of faculty members who have served the Academy for twenty-five years or longer.

8 Frank L. and Helen Childs Boyden Library

William & Geoffrey Platt, 1968; renovation, Architectural Resources Cambridge, 2015

In 1968, Deerfield Academy dedicated the Frank L. Boyden Library to its famous headmaster, who retired that year from the position he had held for sixty-six years. (Helen Childs Boyden's name was added to the library when the science center named in her honor was demolished in 2003.) The library marked the end of an era in more ways than one: not only was it the last building erected under Boyden's leadership, it was also the final project that William and Geoffrey Platt completed for Deerfield, thirty-eight years after their father was first commissioned to design the Main School Building.

The Platt brothers proposed several schematic designs before arriving at the current version. By the late 1950s, when the planning for the library began, Deerfield's central Quad had begun to take shape, defined by the Main School Building and Arms Building on the east, Plunkett Dormitory on the south, and the Memorial Building on the north. The natural location for a library would have been to the west, next to John Williams House and defining the fourth side of a complete quadrangle, but Boyden was extremely fond of the view from the Quad toward the western hills and opposed any encroachment on that vista. Accordingly, the early site plans for the library place it to the west of the Memorial Building (now the Hess Center), but farther north, away from the Quad. The earliest schemes show a low,

Brooke's Garden

Frank L. and Helen Childs Boyden Library

Boyden Library, interior

one-story building, pushed as far to the north as possible in a clear attempt to minimize its impact. Over the course of the design process, the building grew to two stories and moved slightly closer to the Quad, but the principal south facade was always kept farther north than that of the Memorial Building.

As the site plan evolved, so did the architectural style. Early schematic drawings show a Colonial Revival building very much in the same vein as those previously designed by the Platts. In one version, the principal facade is almost identical to that of the Main School Building, except that the two-story portico is replaced by a glassy, one-story entrance pavilion. By 1964, though, the design began to reflect the influence of modernism, with most of the ornament stripped away and the floor plan shaped into an asymmetrical footprint, reminiscent of Walter Gropius's archetypal modernist design of 1925 for the Bauhaus.

The final design for the library returns to the symmetrical Palladian massing established by Charles Platt in the 1930s; however, its austere detailing is without precedent at Deerfield, marking a contrast with the Platts' previous work. The result is a streamlined yet rectilinear aesthetic somewhat reminiscent of art deco design. Compare, for example, the Main School Building: both buildings feature a two-story entrance portico, yet where the earlier version projects from the facade of the building, the library's entrance is recessed within the main volume. Similarly, the Boyden Library abandons the traditional ornament associated with the portico, omitting the bases and capitals from the columns, which are square in plan. The main reading room is a symmetrical wood-paneled room with a fireplace at each end, yet its minimal moldings and flat veneered panels are in stark contrast to the elaborate oak carving and raised paneling of the Caswell Library in the Main School Building.

In 2015, Architectural Resources Cambridge oversaw extensive renovations to the Boyden Library, transforming much of the interior, including downsizing and moving the grand staircase from one side of the building to the other for a more efficient use of space. The overall aesthetic of the refurbished library is perhaps best described as "midcentury modern revival," and ironically, the 2015 work is more characteristic of the 1960s than the original 1968 design was.

9 Longitude Dial

William Andrewes, 2007

Centered directly in front of the Boyden Library sits a remarkable horological instrument known as a Longitude Dial, invented and fabricated by clockmaker William Andrewes.

This dial is one of only a few in existence, each of which Andrewes custom designs for its specific geographic location. Without any moving parts, the ingenious device nonetheless marks time in several ways simultaneously. A projection of the Western Hemisphere is laser etched on the polished stone face of the dial, with Deerfield at the center. The fixed wire gnomon (the cord suspended above the dial) casts a linear shadow onto this face, indicating where noon is at any given moment. The shadow from a gold bead on the gnomon shows the location on the globe where the sun is directly overhead—on the equinoxes, for example, the bead's shadow will track directly along the equator, while on the summer solstice it will follow the Tropic of Cancer. In addition to these latitudes, Deerfield's dial is engraved with a line that the bead's shadow will follow each year on March 1, the day on which the Academy was founded in 1797. Around the perimeter of the dial, the gnomon's shadow passes along a ring of roman and arabic numerals to indicate the hour and minute of local time.

The pedestal is made of Indiana limestone, the same stone used for the exterior trim on many campus buildings. The stone arches are aligned with a large compass rose of several types of colored granite. Narrow slits between the arches allow daylight to penetrate only when the sun is exactly aligned with the cardinal directions. When the sun is due south, the length of the shadow produced indicates the day of the year on a scale engraved in the granite paving.

10 Helen Childs Boyden Science Center

Robertson Ward Jr., 1974; demolished, 2003

Since 1933, science classes at Deerfield had been taught in the Arms Building. By the 1970s, though, science education had evolved to a point where the school deemed a new building necessary. Deerfield named its second science building, completed in 1974, in honor of Helen Childs Boyden, one of the school's most revered teachers and the wife of longtime headmaster Frank Boyden. A Deerfield native, she graduated from Smith College in 1904 and the following year began teaching chemistry and algebra at the Academy. She and Boyden were married in 1907, and they served the school together for more than six decades, until 1968. When Deerfield began planning for the new science building several years later, it was only fitting to name it in Helen's honor and to place the building next to the recently completed Frank L. Boyden Library.

One key educational principle guiding the design for the building was a newly interdisciplinary approach to the sciences: no longer were biology, chemistry, and physics to be taught in isolation from one another. Deerfield's then new headmaster, David Pynchon, declared that "the spaces, too, in which learning takes place will change: the old egg-crate concept of classrooms is giving way to flexible spaces... which might be adjustable to the unknown needs of education of the future." Thus, in addition to five conventional classrooms, the new building featured a vast open laboratory space designed to maximize flexibility and encourage cross-pollination between disciplines.

The building's most glamorous feature was its central planetarium, the second-largest such facility in New England when it was built. In addition to astronomy shows, the school used this versatile space for a wide range of functions, including lectures, meetings, and even theatrical productions.

The Boyden Science Center marked a break with tradition from a stylistic as well as functional standpoint. It was the first new building in seventy years not overseen by Frank Boyden and the first building in forty years not designed by one of the Platts. The architect selected was Robertson Ward Jr., assisted by Timothy Smith (who would go on to design Johnson-Doubleday Dormitory). Their design brought the modernist style to Deerfield for the first time. This approach to design is defined by the rejection of all previous stylistic traditions and by the omission of ornament in favor of pure orthogonal forms and a utilitarian aesthetic inspired by industrial machinery. Even within this radical set of conventions, however, Ward

Longitude Dial

found subtle ways to visually link his design to other buildings on campus. The walls, for example, like those in many of the Platts' designs, were constructed of red brick laid in a Flemish bond pattern. Rising above the otherwise flat roof, the building's dominant feature was a massive pyramid enclosing the internal dome of the planetarium. The pyramid rested on deep concrete beams supported by square piers, four on a side, an arrangement abstractly reminiscent (despite its horizontal proportions) of the adjacent library portico, with its square limestone columns and simplified entablature.

Despite its starkly contrasting architectural style, Ward's design adopted an attitude of modesty in its relation to the rest of the campus. As with the adjacent library, one of the greatest concerns in the schematic design of the Boyden Science Center was to avoid infringing on the view of the western hills. To meet this requirement, Ward and Smith took advantage of the site's topography, which slopes downward away from campus to the north. They sank the building into this hillside, so that

Helen Childs Boyden Science Center, rendering

to the main Quad on the south it presented a single-story facade, while on the north, facing away from campus, two full stories stood above grade. Ward created a bowl-like depression by carving out the earth in front of the building, admitting daylight into the lower-level lab space. A screen of sugar maples softened the rigid geometry of the architecture, so that the building gradually eased into the landscape.

11 Koch Center for Science, Mathematics and Technology

David Childs and Roger Duffy of Skidmore, Owings & Merrill, 2007

By the late 1990s, Deerfield's student body was outgrowing available classroom space, and the school determined that a new math classroom building would be the best way to alleviate the strain on existing facilities. Planning initially focused on a possible addition to the existing Boyden Science Center, but it was eventually decided that the thirty-five-year-old science building should be replaced by a completely new structure that would combine teaching facilities for science, math, and technology. What began as a modest project to create additional math classrooms ultimately became the Koch Center for Science, Mathematics and Technology, an 80,000-square-foot complex, comprising twenty classrooms, lab spaces, a 225-seat auditorium, an astronomy viewing terrace, and a planetarium.

David Koch (class of 1958) provided funding for the project, and to design the building, the Academy selected Koch's contemporary at Deerfield, David Childs (class of 1959) of Skidmore, Owings & Merrill. This was Childs's third project at Deerfield and his second with Koch as patron. In 1995, Childs had designed the Koch Natatorium, and in 1998, a pair of dormitories on the eastern side of the campus.

Childs's first two projects at Deerfield take the campus's Colonial Revival architecture as their aesthetic starting point. For the Koch Center, he worked with partner Roger Duffy to develop a completely novel stylistic idiom. Duffy, who had a history of seeking out unorthodox collaborators, called in astronomers, geologists, and several artists to consult on the design. The building's style is modernist, but it stands in sharp contrast to the modernism employed by Ward in the earlier science building. In fact, the stylistic relationship between the two science buildings is surprisingly analogous to that between Charles Platt's Main School Building and its predecessor by Peabody & Stearns: they nominally share an architectural style, but they are polar opposites in character—one disciplined and orderly, the other playful and capricious.

With the exception of the pyramid, the lines of Ward's science building had been completely orthogonal, in the tradition of early modernists like Walter Gropius and Mies van der Rohe. The layout and arrangement of functions was immediately legible. By contrast, the dynamic Koch Center defies easy comprehension (and description), its character shifting from one moment to the next with an almost Baroque sense of drama. From certain angles, its flat roofs lend it a sense of repose, while from others, the unpredictable curvatures of its brick walls seem to put the whole building in motion, a reference to the nearby Deerfield River.

The interior is similarly fluid. The swerves and intersections of hallways bring to mind the unplanned streets of a medieval Italian hill town—an association enhanced by the exposed brick walls and the availability of cappuccino at the building's Louis Café. In place of a piazza, the corridors converge on a central three-story atrium. Sinuous contours of corridors and balconies on all three levels are highlighted by curving illumination panels set into the floors and ceilings and a skylight above inspired by an analemma—a curve that represents the movement of celestial bodies. The floor of the atrium is inscribed with a star map that is reflected with pinhole lights on the ceiling; with the stars of the Southern Hemisphere embedded in the floor and those of the Northern Hemisphere above, the aesthetic is simultaneously organic and high tech.

Perhaps the most striking aspect of the Koch Center's design is the flamboyant visual contrast it makes with the otherwise stylistically harmonious campus. The

OVERLEAF **Koch Center**

Koch Center, interior

Boyden Science Center had been exceptional at Deerfield for its modernist style, but even so, it had been designed not to draw attention to itself. The Koch Center does just the opposite.

Apart from its eccentric stylistic sensibility, the Koch Center is notable for its numerous green design features, demonstrating Deerfield's increasing emphasis on environmental sustainability. The building is constructed with locally sourced bricks, double-glazed windows, rooftop solar panels, and a green roof that reduces stormwater runoff. These and other measures earned the Koch Center a LEED (Leadership in Energy and Environmental Design) Gold certification from the U.S. Green Building Council.

WALK TWO

Beyond the Classroom: Buildings for the Arts, Athletics, and Communal Living

12 Hess Center for the Arts
13 Two Earlier Activities Buildings *(demolished)*
14 Dewey Dormitory and Health Center
15 Dining Hall
16 American Elm Trees
17 Lower Level
18 Headmaster's Field
19 Athletic Center
20 Hammerschlag Boathouse *(off campus)*

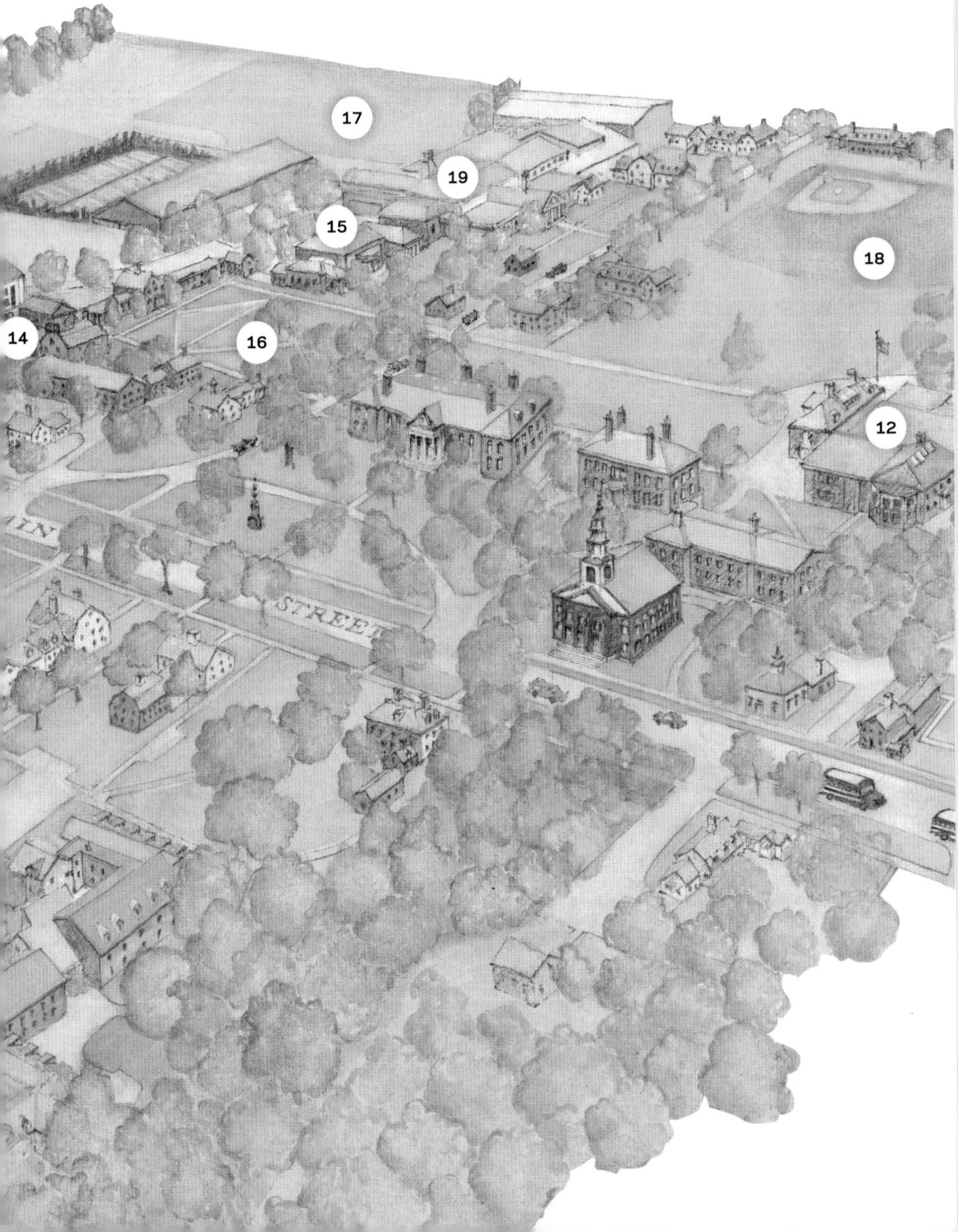
17
19
15
18
14
16
12

WALK TWO

Beyond the Classroom: Buildings for the Arts, Athletics, and Communal Living

In Walk One, we considered all of Deerfield's primary academic buildings, their ties to the colonial history of the surrounding village and valley, and the singular role of Headmaster Frank Boyden and his architects in shaping the design of the campus. Walk Two will broaden our view to include a diverse group of spaces beyond the school's classrooms. These facilities for athletic and artistic pursuits as well as residential life are nonetheless essential to the education of Deerfield students and the formation of the school's strong sense of community.

We begin on the northern side of campus with the Hess Center for the Arts, which houses spaces for both performing and fine arts, as well as the school's main auditorium. We then proceed south through the Quad and across Albany Road, passing by the sites where two historic multipurpose buildings once stood. After pausing at the original Health Center, we move on to the Dining Hall, the building that brings the students together with the greatest frequency. From there, we descend the hill to the playing fields of the Lower Level before ending with the expansive Athletic Center.

These buildings house a wide range of activities, but whether it be a hockey game, a chamber music concert, a theatrical production, or simply a group conversation around a dinner table, they all share emphasis on collaboration, teamwork, and community. The buildings in this walk exist to teach Deerfield students how to live and work together to achieve what would be impossible individually.

To a large degree, this communal ideal is reflected in the architecture of the buildings themselves, where the designs of different architects work with one another to form an artistic ensemble much greater than the sum of its parts. Accordingly, this chapter will continue to focus not only on individual buildings but also on the relationships between buildings across time as well as physical space. It is especially fitting that two of the buildings discussed in this walk, the arts and athletics centers, are in fact composites, comprising of multiple buildings constructed over a period of decades by different architects.

12 Hess Center for the Arts

a. Memorial Building, William & Geoffrey Platt, 1951
b. Hilson Art Gallery, William & Geoffrey Platt, 1955
c. Reed Center for the Arts, Tony Atkin (Atkin Olshin Schade Architects), 1989; renovation, Architectural Resources Cambridge, 2014
d. Reid Black Box Theater, Tony Atkin (Atkin Olshin Schade Architects), 1989, renovation, 1993
e. Dance Studio, Architectural Resources Cambridge, 2001
f. Von Auersperg Gallery, Architectural Resources Cambridge, 2014
g. Wachsmann Concert Hall, Architectural Resources Cambridge, 2014

During the past half century, the arts at Deerfield have transformed from peripheral club activities to central components of the school's educational mission, fully integrated into the curriculum. The Academy now offers courses in drawing, painting, photography, videography, architecture, music, theater, and dance. The home for these pursuits is the recently renovated Hess Center for the Arts. This large complex is in fact a conglomeration of seven buildings, designed by three architectural firms over the course of more than five decades.

The oldest portion of the Hess Center is the Memorial Building, completed in 1951 and dedicated to Deerfield alumni who died during the Second World War. The centerpiece of this building is an auditorium large enough to accommodate the entire student body and faculty. This space is used for music, theater, and dance performances as well as weekly all-school meetings and is known simply as the Large Auditorium. A generous lobby faces the Quad and doubles as a student lounge and reception hall. The second floor served as a library until the current Boyden Library was completed in 1968.

On its completion, the Memorial Building provided dedicated spaces for the performing arts, including a theater shop and music practice rooms. For the first time, activities that had previously met in dispersed and makeshift facilities were

OPPOSITE **Memorial Building (now part of the Hess Center for the Arts)**

Henry Varnum Poor tiles

centralized in one location. In 1969, the Academy added a fine arts department led by painter and educator Daniel Hodermarsky, and the Memorial Building basement was renovated to include art studios. These facilities established the core around which the modern arts center would eventually grow.

In designing the Memorial Building, architects William and Geoffrey Platt were following through on a plan first conceived by their father, Charles, in the 1930s. The elder Platt intended that a major structure be built on this site, at the northern edge of campus, directly across from Plunkett Dormitory, which had been built in 1926 on the south side of Albany Road. These two buildings, then, along with his Main School Building and Arms Building to the east, would define three sides of a large quadrangle (the west side remaining open). Charles Platt originally proposed a dormitory for this site, but that was never built; as early as 1942, William and Geoffrey began sketching designs for an "activities building" instead. By 1949, this concept had evolved into the final design for the Memorial Building.

Architecturally, the Memorial Building carries forward the Colonial Revival style that Charles established with the Main School Building, Arms Building, and Gymnasium in the early 1930s. Built of red brick with painted wood trim, the principal facade follows a similarly Palladian composition: a rectangular volume capped by a hipped roof and marked at the center by a classical temple front. Whereas the temple front of the Main School Building is a projecting portico with freestanding columns, at the Memorial Building it is flattened against the facade, the pediment supported by brick pilasters (square columns engaged with the wall). Three central pairs of French doors open onto the spacious lobby, focused around a fireplace. The lobby walls were, until recently, adorned with scenic wallpaper depicting late-eighteenth-century views of New York City. This wallpaper, the gift of Deerfield parent Joseph Reed in 1957, had been salvaged from a New York City bank and was restored and installed in 1967.

William and Geoffrey also designed the first addition to the Memorial Building—the Hilson Gallery—in 1955. This one-room pavilion is grafted onto the west side of the auditorium with a public entrance facing south toward the Quad, but set back so as not to compete with the principal facade of the Memorial Building. To maximize wall space for the display of exhibits, fenestration is limited to a single large window in the west wall. This could have resulted in too plain a facade on the south side facing the Quad, but for a pair of decorative panels set into the exterior wall flanking the entrance. Consisting of hand-painted tiles by Henry Varnum Poor, a celebrated painter and muralist who executed several large commissions for various US government agencies, these panels represent the sciences and humanities. A third panel, depicting scenes of Academy life, originally surrounded the fireplace inside the gallery. These tiles were moved and reconfigured in the most recent renovation.

In 1989, the Reed Center for the Arts was added to the east of the auditorium. The arts addition was made possible by a donation from the Reed family, whose four sons had attended Deerfield. Their father, Joseph Reed, described in his *New York Times* obituary as "a hustling theatrical entrepreneur in New York, a land developer in Florida, a diplomat in Paris, a newspaper reporter, art collector, author and loving compiler of word games and cryptograms," was a fascinating character who grew close to the Boydens and would stay with them when he visited. Reed donated to Deerfield a copy of John James Audubon's 1838 "double elephant" folio of *Birds of America*, one of the most valuable books in the world, and then agreed when the Academy decided to sell the book in order to fund the arts center project.

Designed by Tony Atkin of Atkin Olshin Schade Architects, a firm that has worked with many academic institutions and focused on renovations of historically significant structures, the new wing created space for new art studios, music rehearsal rooms, and on the upper floor, an architecture studio. Despite being designed forty years after the Memorial Building, the Reed Center's architecture was remarkably compatible. The scale, facade composition, and hipped roof echoed the overall forms of the earlier structure, and Atkin employed classical details that harmonized with those of the Platts without strictly replicating them. Most of these elements were sacrificed during the most recent renovation, which grafted a new addition onto the main facade of the Reed Center.

Atkin also added the Reid Black Box Theater directly north of the Hilson Art Gallery. With this addition, the gallery took on an added function as the theater lobby, which gives greater visibility to the artwork displayed there. The theater itself is a cubic space with a central stage surrounded by seating on four sides. As the name suggests, the interior is completely black to provide an almost invisible backdrop for the sets and theatrical lighting. The architecture of the exterior is nearly as inconspicuous: a plain brick box neatly tucked away behind the gallery.

Deerfield's dance program received its own dedicated studio in 2001 with an addition to the rear of the Large Auditorium designed by Architectural Resources Cambridge (ARC). This addition has a somewhat more elaborate architectural

Reed Center for the Arts (facade demolished)

character than the Reid Black Box Theater, adopting an abstracted Colonial Revival style in keeping with the rest of the complex. The interior features a large open area for dance rehearsals with raised tiers for audience seating along the south side.

In 2014, the arts complex underwent another major renovation and expansion and was renamed the Hess Center for the Arts, after the principal donors. This project, also designed by ARC, included two large additions. On the west side of the auditorium, the Hilson Art Gallery was augmented by a second, larger display space, the von Auersperg Gallery. On the east side, the Reed Center wing was doubled in size to house the new Elizabeth Wachsman Concert Hall. These twin additions stand directly in front of the two older wings, effectively replacing the Colonial Revival facades designed by Atkin and the Platts with minimalist flat-roofed blocks. Unlike ARC's dance studio of a decade earlier, these highly visible additions make a dramatic departure from the stylistic language of the rest of the ensemble, adopting a brand of modernism reminiscent of the 1974 Boyden Science Center.

13 Two Earlier Activities Buildings

a. Town School and Grange Hall, builder unknown, 1842; moved and renovated (with portico addition) by Deerfield Academy as Girls Club, 1912; demolished, 1951

b. The Barn, construction date and builder unknown; renovated by Deerfield Academy as a gym, theater, and activity center, 1924; demolished, 1976

As noted above, when the Memorial Building was constructed in 1951, it established the northern edge of a large quadrangle, bounded by the Main School Building and Arms Building to the east and Plunkett Dormitory to the south. The fourth side of this space remained open, preserving Boyden's cherished view of the western hills. In order for this quadrangle to be fully realized, however, it needed to be cleared of one significant intrusion, a wood-frame building known as the Girls Club, which since 1912 had stood immediately to the west of the Main School Building—right in the middle of the newly established Quad. Although from a campus planning standpoint it was right to remove this building, it is worth remembering it here because of its historical and architectural significance.

The Girls Club building was originally constructed as the town school. It was built in 1842 on the site currently occupied by the town post office and served as a schoolhouse until 1874, when it was purchased from the town for use as a Grange hall. During the late nineteenth and early twentieth centuries, the building served a number of functions, including as shops, offices, library, and post office.

In 1912, Deerfield resident Jennie Maria Arms Sheldon purchased the old building and donated it to the Academy for use as an academic and social center for the school's female students. Jennie had been one of the first women to enroll as a student at MIT, where her interest was zoology and entomology. She subsequently worked for many years with zoologist and paleontologist Alpheus Hyatt at the Boston Society of Natural History and for thirteen years taught natural science

Girls Club (demolished)

at a school in Boston. After moving to Deerfield to marry George Sheldon in 1897, Jennie became a significant patron of the Academy. (See Walk Four, page 43.) She made her first modest contribution to the school in the very early days of Boyden's tenure as headmaster, when the jury was still out as to whether the school would survive or not. "Something has lifted the spirit of this community," she told Boyden when she offered to purchase new baseball uniforms for the school, quickly adding, "but don't tell anyone I gave the money for it." Jennie went on to give much larger—and very public—gifts, most notably funding the construction of the Arms Building. Purchasing a building for use by Deerfield Academy's girls was an indication of her passion for women's education.

Deerfield moved this building up the hill to its new site and remodeled it, inside and out. The Girls Club contained a dining room and kitchen, classrooms for teaching "domestic science," and the school store. Over time, the building served a variety of functions, hosting special dinners, receptions, trustee meetings, parties, and even theatrical productions that were sometimes staged outdoors on the front portico.

The building's original design was simple: a two-story wooden box similar to many of the houses in town, with a front facade consisting of five bays of double-hung windows and a central entrance. Its distinctive features were the substantial wood pilasters at each corner, which supported an entablature running the full width of the main facade. These classical elements were specifically Greek in style,

The Barn (demolished)

a mode of design that was highly fashionable in the United States from the 1820s through the 1840s. (The old town hall on Memorial Street provides another good example.) The details in this case were modeled after the Choragic Monument of Thrasyllus, built in the fourth century BC at the base of the Acropolis in Athens to commemorate the ancient Greek chorus leader Thrasyllus, who led his singing group to victory at a festival competition. This was among many classical Greek designs popularized in the United States in the early nineteenth century through pattern books written by architects such as Asher Benjamin, the designer of Deerfield's original Academy Building. Lamentably, the Turks destroyed the Monument of Thrasyllus during the Greek War of Independence in the 1820s, so by the time its details were adapted to American buildings such as Deerfield's town school, its memory survived only in books like those published by Benjamin.

The 1912 remodeling dramatically altered the building's appearance, but in a way that preserved and extended the Greek Revival style of the original design. The main facade was reconfigured with larger windows and a two-story portico was added, along with a pair of dormers. The portico columns and entablature carefully matched those of the original structure, and the new windows and doors were likewise executed in a compatible style. Indeed, the building in its new configuration was as attractive as the original, if not more so, and it is regrettable that it was demolished rather than moved (a second time) in 1951.

At the opposite end of the architectural spectrum from the refinement of the Girls Club was a structure known simply as "the Barn"—something decidedly more Spartan than Athenian. This former horse barn was purchased by the Academy in

1924, and after some rudimentary renovation work—some of which was done by the students—it provided a rustic but generous space that could be used for a variety of functions.

Until the construction of the Gymnasium in 1932, the Barn was the school's only athletics facility. Students also used it as a rehearsal and performance space for theater and music, especially the most popular ensemble of that era, the Glee Club. Finally, the Barn provided a venue for student entertainment, such as regular movie screenings.

In 1976, after a half century of use, Deerfield demolished the Barn. Thirteen years later, DeNunzio Dormitory was built on the site where it once stood.

14 Dewey Dormitory and Health Center

William & Geoffrey Platt, 1948

After the completion in the early 1930s of Charles Platt's transformational projects, the Main School Building, Arms Building, and the Gymnasium, the Academy's next priority was to build an infirmary. Platt died in 1933, however, raising the question as to who would succeed him as the school's principal architect. There were several eager contenders. In 1936, the distinguished Boston firm of Cram and Ferguson (which had recently designed an infirmary for Choate) submitted proposals for a small infirmary, and in 1941, J. R. Hampson of Pittsfield, Massachusetts, submitted designs for a much larger facility. In the end, the Academy chose to retain Platt's sons, William and Geoffrey, who had assisted their father in his work at Deerfield during his last years. The infirmary was eventually built to their design in 1948, along with a new dining hall. These were the first of fifteen buildings the Platt brothers would complete for Deerfield over the next two decades.

The Platts drew their inspiration for the infirmary—as well as several subsequent Academy buildings—from early American houses. The infirmary thus could be considered the prototype for the five Colonial Revival dormitories built in the 1950s, as well as the more recent Harold Smith Dormitory. (See Walk Three, pages 120 and 139.) Whereas those later dormitories were clad in wood clapboards, the Health Center was built of red brick, matching the palette that Charles Platt had so convincingly established.

The inspiration for the Health Center's design was a brick house at 338 Main Street in Charleston, New Hampshire, which dates from about 1823. It is not clear why the Platts selected this house as the model; however, three years earlier, Henry Flynt, then president of the Academy's board of trustees, had restored another brick house, the 1799 Asa Stebbins House, which lay just north of campus. This project may have sparked a general interest in Federal-style brick residential architecture. Among the details the Platts derived from the Charleston house are the prominent chimneys that emerge from the gable end parapets, as well as elegant arched doors with sidelights and an elliptical fanlight, a celebrated hallmark of the Federal style.

Dewey Dormitory

However, Dewey's handsome design and solid construction were not enough to save it for posterity. Following completion of the D.S. Chen Health and Wellness Center in 2019, the Academy approved plans to replace Dewey with a new dormitory.

15 Dining Hall

William & Geoffrey Platt, 1948; addition, Tony Atkin (Atkin Olshin Schade Architects), 1992; renovation and addition, Thomas Douglas, 2011

Communal dining has long been one of the defining traditions of life at Deerfield. Headmaster Boyden believed in bringing the entire school together "just as you have your family together once a day." It was Boyden who initiated many of the dining traditions that remain hallmarks of dining at Deerfield. He mandated that all students take turns waiting on tables, and he set aside time at the end of meals for general announcements and for the recognition of student accomplishments. Most importantly, he established dining as a central means of building community and keeping a finger on the pulse of the student body as a whole. Seating is assigned, and a faculty member heads each ten-person table, ensuring that students will have the opportunity to get to know teachers and other students with whom they might not otherwise cross paths. Today, the school maintains seven formal sit-down meals per week (four lunches and three dinners), which all students are required to attend.

Since 1920, when roughly 140 students attended the school, meals had been served in a large room added to the rear of Hitchcock House. This space could comfortably seat only about seventy people at once, however, and as enrollment grew, a much larger building was required so that the entire school could dine together in the same room. The Academy completed this new building in 1948, the same year the Health Center opened. William and Geoffrey Platt served as the architects for both projects, though the Dining Hall was by far the more substantial of the two commissions.

The Platts' design for this building is simple and logical: A grand, high-ceilinged dining room in the center, almost a square in plan, flanked by lower wings housing a lobby to the east and a kitchen to the west. To the north and south of the lobby are two intimately scaled dining rooms suitable for small dinners for faculty, trustees, or student groups. The east and west walls of the main dining room are symmetrical, with four pairs of paneled doors leading to the lobby and kitchen, respectively. The doors are framed by a series of fluted Doric pilasters that are set on a continuous chair rail. In the original design, a single large semicircular bay protruded from the south side of the dining room, with windows looking out over the playing fields of the Lower Level.

As part of a 1992 renovation, architect Tony Atkin (who also designed the Reed Center for the Arts) matched this bay with one of equal size on the north side, framing it with a pair of monumental Doric columns. Between these columns hangs a row of flags reflecting the nationalities of the student body. In 2010, a fire severely damaged the Dining Hall, but the building was quickly restored under the

Dining Hall, interior

Dining Hall

Dining Hall, lobby interior

direction of Northampton architect Thomas Douglas, who took the opportunity to replace the south bay with an even larger one, significantly increasing capacity. Like Atkin before him, Douglas took pains to match the detailing of the original building, although the new bay may appear overscaled to some.

The Dining Hall lobby is notable for its scenic wallpaper, which was printed from wood blocks made by the French manufacturer Zuber & Cie in 1853. It depicts historical episodes from the American Revolution, fancifully superimposed on distinctive (yet unrelated) American natural settings, such as Niagara Falls and the Natural Bridge. The surrender of Lord Cornwallis at Yorktown, Virginia, for example, is shown inexplicably with the dramatic cliffs of West Point in the background. This

wallpaper was donated by the Reed family, which also donated the wallpaper that once adorned the Memorial Hall lobby.

16 American Elm Trees

On the lawn directly in front of the Dining Hall stand two of the last large American elms (*Ulmus americana*) in Deerfield. They are estimated to be between 120 and 150 years old. Elms are prized for their graceful vaselike form and spreading canopy, and they were once the dominant shade tree in towns throughout New England. This pair provides a glimpse of the way the entire campus and town looked generations

American elms on Plunkett Quadrangle

ago: photographs from the nineteenth and early twentieth centuries depict majestic, cathedral-like spaces created by hundreds of massive elms planted in rows along both sides of the Street and Albany Road. (See pages 18–19.)

Tragically, almost all of these trees have been lost to an aggressive fungal pathogen known as Dutch elm disease, which was accidentally introduced to the United States in 1928 and has now killed the vast majority of the country's elms. Deerfield's remaining elms are protected to a degree by regular injections of a fungicide that significantly reduce the risk of infection. In recent years, disease-resistant American elm cultivars have been identified and propagated, raising the prospect that these spectacular trees could one day return to Deerfield.

17 Lower Level

At the west end of Albany Road, a path leads down the steep slope to the playing fields of the Lower Level. This broad expanse of fields, which surround the campus on three sides, is part of the Deerfield River floodplain. It provides an ideal setting for athletic contests, especially because its proximity to the campus encourages students to attend games. The one drawback is that the Deerfield River tends to flood during the early spring; in some years, this has put the entire Lower Level underwater just when teams need to start practicing for the season.

In addition to playing fields, the Lower Level is home to the Morsman Tennis Pavilion (to the south of the Natatorium) and the track (northwest of the Koch Center for Science, Mathematics and Technology).

Partway down the path to the Lower Level is a promontory known as Gordie's Overlook, named in memory of Lynn Gordon "Gordie" Bailey Jr. (class of 2004). At Deerfield, Gordie excelled in athletics, music, and drama and was remembered for his leadership, compassion, and good humor. He died in his first month at the University of Colorado, Boulder, of an alcohol overdose as part of a fraternity hazing ritual. His family created the Gordie Foundation—now the Gordie Center for Substance Abuse Prevention at the University of Virginia—to prevent similar tragedies.

18 Headmaster's Field

Since the early twentieth century, the varsity baseball field has occupied a place of honor at the west end of the Quad. Headmaster Boyden played on Deerfield's baseball team until he was thirty-five and coached until he was nearly eighty. Because of his fondness for the sport, he kept the field in this prominent location rather than down on the Lower Level. Headmaster's Field, as it is now known, underwent an extensive renovation in 2012 to bring it up to Major League standards.

Beyond left field is a grove of locust trees framing the Huffard Garden, a memorial to Wick Huffard (class of 2003), who died in a car accident the year after he graduated from Deerfield. Huffard aspired to be an architect, and an annual

Lower Level, from Gordie's Overlook

Lower Level flooding following Hurricane Irene, August 2011

Headmaster's Field

architecture lecture at Deerfield is named in his memory. The garden features several historic millstones that were collected by Deerfield parent Howard Howland Brown and donated to the Academy in 1992. Other stones from this collection can be found throughout the campus. (The stone pictured here was made in 1836 for a cider mill in Amherst, Massachusetts.)

19 Athletic Center

a. East Gym, Charles A. Platt, 1932; Greer Store renovation, Kuhn Riddle Architects, 2010
b. Hockey Rink, William & Geoffrey Platt, 1957; demolished, 2017
c. West Gym, William & Geoffrey Platt, 1963
d. Koch Natatorium, David Childs (Skidmore, Owings & Merrill), 1995
e. Robert M. Dewey Jr. '49 Squash Center, Architectural Resources Cambridge, 2007
f. David H. Koch Field House, Class of 1993 Hockey Rink, and Morsman Tennis Pavilion, Sasaki Associates, 2018

Like the Hess Center for the Arts, Deerfield's Athletic Center is an amalgam of spaces that were designed and constructed by various architects over many

Cider stone
OVERLEAF **East Gym**

22

Greer Store interior

decades. It represents not only the expansion of the school but also changes in architectural style over time, and it provides an illustration of the way in which new additions can be designed to harmonize or contrast with an existing architectural context.

Boyden is said to have initiated Deerfield's athletics program on his first day as headmaster in 1902, announcing to the handful of students that instead of going straight home after classes finished, they were all going to go outside and play football. Soon he had Deerfield's students competing against other local schools, often playing alongside them to help fill out the ranks. For the next six decades, on top of his duties as headmaster, Boyden served as the school's head coach for football, baseball, and basketball. He employed athletics pragmatically as a kind of controlled outlet for the potentially unruly energy of his adolescent students, but he also sought to build character by emphasizing sportsmanship. "We may wish [the students] were interested in other things," he commented, "but we must meet existing conditions, and since they will have athletic sports anyway, let us control them and make them a moral force."

Boyden's high regard for the role of athletics at Deerfield is evident in his first major capital campaign of 1929. The printed fundraising brochure proposed

East Gym rendering

to double the size of the campus with the addition of three buildings: a gym, a new academic building (the Main School Building), and a dormitory, in that order. Furthermore, he proposed to spend an equal amount on the construction of the gym as would be spent on the school's sole academic building. The resulting building, forming the core of the present-day Athletic Center and now known as the Class of 1953 Gymnasium, was designed by Charles Platt and completed in 1932. Considering that this is one of three buildings Platt designed almost simultaneously, it is worth comparing it with his other two contributions to the Deerfield campus: the Main School Building and the Arms Building.

The first thing to note about the gym is its location. Whereas Platt placed the Main School Building and Arms Building on the most prominent possible site, facing directly onto the Town Common, he set the gym back to the west, more than halfway down Albany Road. Over the past eighty years, a number of major buildings have filled out that western end of campus, but in 1932 it would have seemed rather remote. This placement allowed the building to achieve the necessary mass without overwhelming the town center or upstaging the smaller-scaled academic buildings.

Beyond the inconspicuous siting of the gym, Platt went to great effort to minimize its apparent scale. Because the basketball court required the highest ceiling—and therefore the tallest roof—Platt pushed this to the rear, screening it from view with a long band of single-story spaces. He capped these with a flat roof so that, despite their large floor area, they would maintain a low profile. The Kravis Arena, a room of graceful yet understated classical design that was originally the swimming pool, occupies the west wing. The east wing houses the ever-popular student snack bar, the Greer Store. In between these two wings is a wood-paneled trophy room, where a large brass medallion bearing the school seal is set into the floor. School tradition holds that no one may step on the seal.

As with his other buildings at Deerfield, Platt gave the gym a classical design, loosely participating in the Colonial Revival tradition and built of red brick with limestone trim. Like the Main School Building, the gym's facade follows a Palladian composition: a projecting classical temple front at the center flanked by symmetrical wings. The low, horizontal proportions of the building, along with its extensive use of arches, recall sixteenth-century Italian villa designs, especially Andrea Palladio's Villa Emo and Villa Barbaro, and Giulio Romano's Palazzo del Te. Where the portico of the Main School Building employs the Ionic order, the gym opts for the Tuscan order, which, with its simpler detailing and stout proportions, is traditionally associated with strength and is therefore an appropriate expression for a gymnasium.

In 1957, Deerfield constructed a detached ice hockey rink following a rather utilitarian (though still abstractly Palladian) design by William and Geoffrey Platt. The rink was situated to the west of the gym designed by their father. In 1963, the same firm designed an addition to fill in the gap between the old gym and the rink. The architecturally undistinguished hockey rink was demolished to make way for a new rink and field house designed by Sasaki Associates (discussed on page 99).

David Childs (class of 1959) is responsible for a more noteworthy addition to the gym complex in 1995. This was Childs's first project for Deerfield—he would go on to design two dormitories and oversee the design of the Koch Center for Science,

Koch Natatorium, tower detail
OPPOSITE **Koch Natatorium**

Koch Natatorium, interior

14"

Class of 1993 Hockey Rink

Mathematics and Technology. Now chairman emeritus at the firm of Skidmore, Owings & Merrill, Childs is perhaps best known as the architect for the new One World Trade Center in New York City.

The centerpiece of this project was the Koch Natatorium, which has an Olympic-sized pool and a diving well. This monumental wing follows the axis of symmetry established in the original gym, extending south toward the Lower Level tennis courts. Childs creates a spectacular interior space for the pools, lit by a series of circular clerestory windows and spanned by exposed timber trusses. A dramatic cupola admits light into a central stair between the pools and the old gym.

On the exterior, Childs enlivens the great mass of the natatorium with decorative brickwork, using blind arches to visually link the addition to Platt's original design. A series of outdoor terraces afford sweeping views out over the Lower Level. As the grade drops away to the south, a massive, rusticated plinth emerges from the hillside to support the natatorium, with symmetrical exterior staircases descending to the Lower Level on either side. Viewed from the playing fields below, it is an unexpectedly monumental gesture, a sort of Medici fortress presiding over the tennis courts.

In 2007, ARC designed another addition to house the Dewey Squash Courts. This facility, which includes ten international squash courts, sits just to the west of the natatorium and matches it in size. In the abstract, the two buildings provide an interesting comparison: separated by only twenty years, they nonetheless embody opposite philosophies and aesthetics. The natatorium explores a wide range of ornamental forms, especially in its decorative brickwork, whereas the squash courts are uncompromisingly minimalist. Where the natatorium is firmly rooted in architectural history, the squash courts eschew any pre-twentieth-century historical precedent. In a poetic visual parallel to this, the natatorium celebrates its massive foundation, while the cantilevered glass curtain wall of the squash courts appears to hover above the ground. One seems solid and permanent, the other light and transient.

Sasaki Associates designed the most recent addition to Deerfield's Athletic Center, a massive replacement for the old ice hockey rink. The new 130,000-square-foot wing features not only the new Class of 1993 Hockey Rink but also the David H. Koch Field House containing an elevated track and a 20,000-square-foot synthetic turf field. Additional facilities include rowing tanks, a puck shooting room, a golf simulator room, new locker rooms, and a variety of spaces for meetings and events.

David H. Koch Field House, Dewey Squash Courts, and Koch Natatorium

Some unusual constraints shaped the design and layout of the addition: the floodplain to the south, a cemetery to the west, dormitories to the north, and the existing gymnasiums to the east. Ultimately, the excavation of 36,000 cubic yards of soil allowed Sasaki to embed the lower portion of the structure below ground and to align the building perpendicular to Albany Road. This plan also allowed for a front hallway to run the length of the building and for a lobby that is accessible from the main doors on the third floor and that leads to a central stairway and the hockey rink below. The addition, the squash courts, and the older gymnasiums were then connected through a central spine to form the Athletics Complex.

Concurrently with this addition, the Academy built a vast metal "pavilion" (covering approximately an acre) to enclose a half dozen existing tennis courts. Within this climate-controlled facility, Deerfield's tennis players are no longer subjected to the vagaries of the New England weather. Ultimately, the appeal of these recent buildings is in the state-of-the-art athletics facilities they contain. These are intended not just to give Deerfield's athletics teams a competitive edge over those of other schools but also to give the Academy itself an advantage in the equally fierce competition to attract the most talented and accomplished students.

20 Hammerschlag Boathouse

Architectural Resources Cambridge, 2005

One athletics facility not to be found on campus is the Hammerschlag Boathouse. The Deerfield River is not large enough for rowing, so crew teams travel by bus over the Pocumtuck Ridge to practice and race on the Connecticut River. For many years, rowing shells were stored in an old tobacco barn—an arrangement reminiscent of the rustic athletics facilities of the early Boyden years. In 2005, however, the

Hammerschlag Boathouse

Academy commissioned ARC to design a new boathouse on a site just up the river from the old barn.

ARC was well qualified for the task, having designed new boathouses or renovated old ones for several other schools and colleges, including Princeton, Exeter, and Boston University. Whereas these earlier projects created, or extended, a clubhouse aesthetic, Deerfield's boathouse is stylistically reminiscent of its agrarian predecessor and the other barns that punctuate the surrounding farmland: The timber-frame structure is clad in vertical boards and protected by a metal roof. Large sliding barn doors give access to three bays of boat storage, which are organized like a basilica, with a tall central "nave" flanked by side aisles that are low enough to accommodate a row of small clerestory windows above.

WALK THREE

Finding Home: the Development of the Modern Dormitory

21 **John Williams House**

22 **Cottonwood Tree** *(removed)*

23 **Early Dormitories**

- **a. Boyden Hall (a.k.a. Old Dorm)** *(demolished)*
- **b. Plunkett Dormitory (a.k.a. New Dorm)** *(demolished)*

24 **Three Italianate Houses**

- **a. Bewkes House**
- **b. Haynes House**
- **c. Ashley House** *(demolished)*

25 **Midcentury Colonial Revival Dormitories**

- **a. Scaife Dormitory**
- **b. Mather Dormitory**
- **c. Pocumtuck Dormitory**
- **d. Field Dormitory**
- **e. McAlister Dormitory**

26 **Barton Dormitory**

27 **Dormitory Quadrangles**

- **a. Johnson and Doubleday Dormitories**
- **b. Rosenwald-Shumway Dormitory**
- **c. DeNunzio Dormitory**
- **d. John Louis Dormitory**
- **e. Louis Marx Dormitory**

28 **Recent Colonial Revival Dormitories**

- **a. Harold Webster Smith Dormitory**
- **b. O'Byrne Curtis Dormitory**

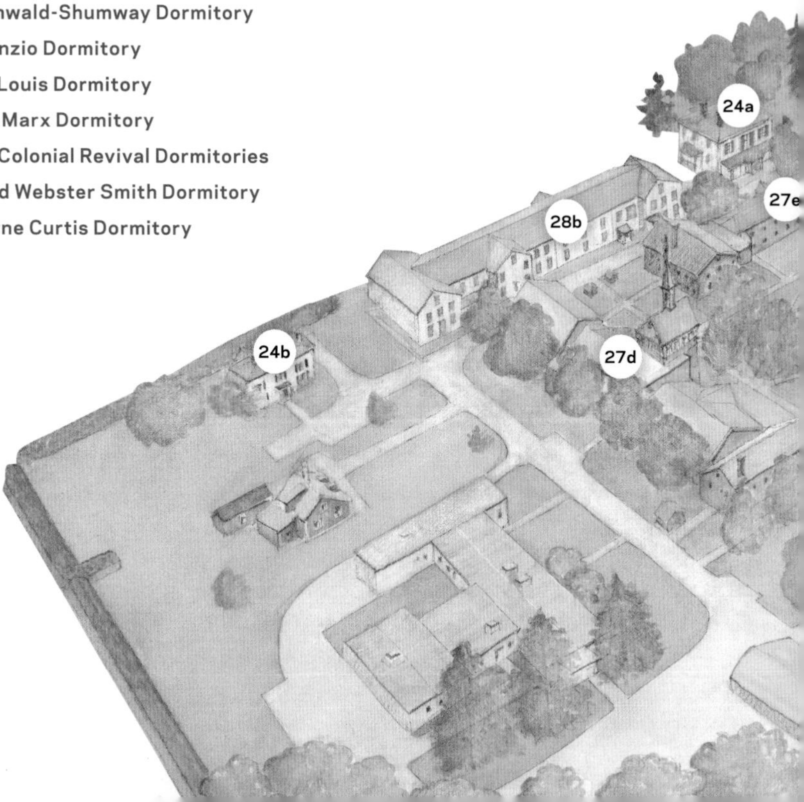

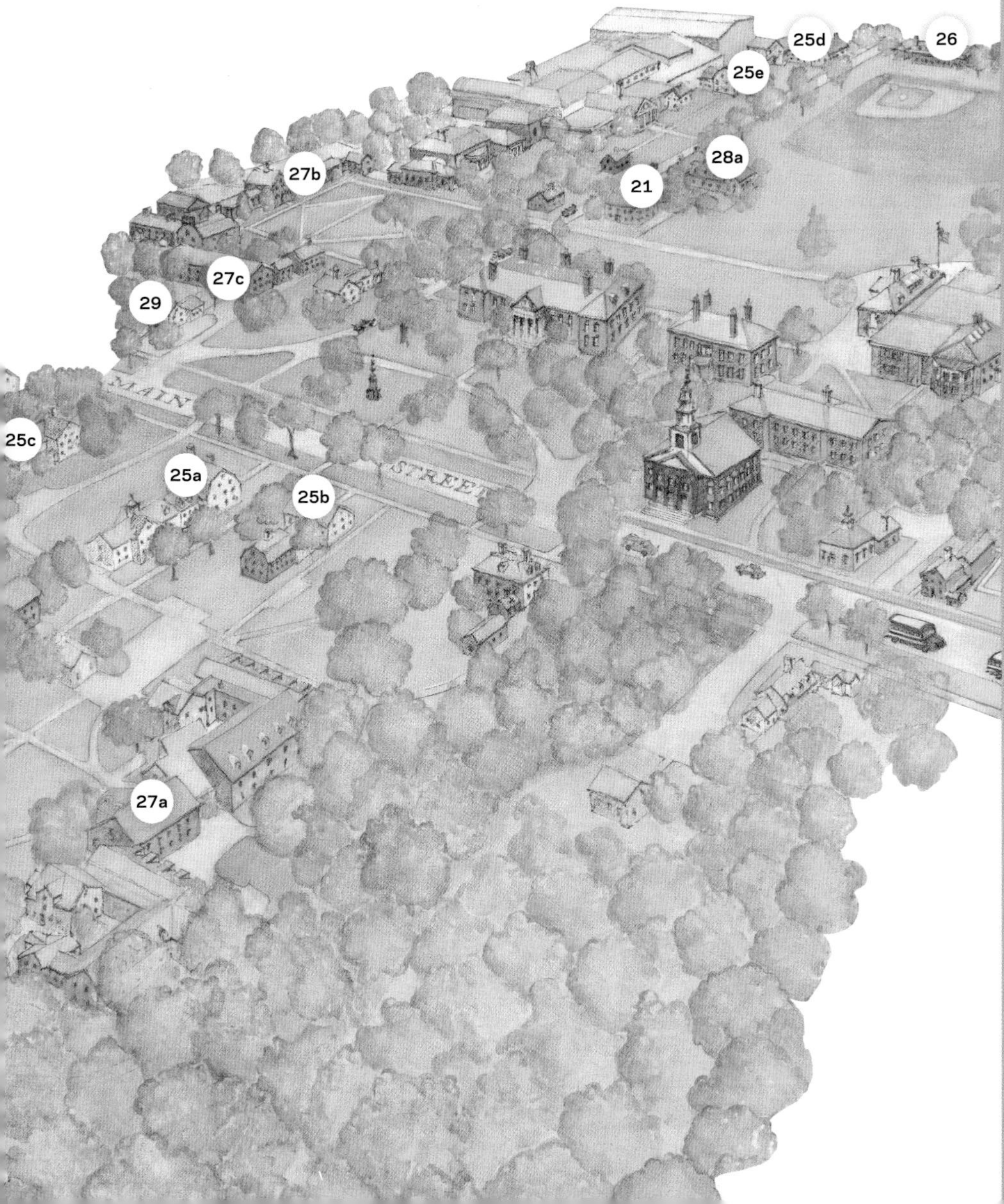
25d
26
25e
28a
27b
21
27c
29
25c
25a
25b
27a
MAIN
STREET

Finding Home: the Development of the Modern Dormitory

When Deerfield Academy first opened its doors in 1799, two-thirds of its approximately seventy students came from afar, most from other towns in western Massachusetts but some from Vermont and even as far away as Albany, New York (probably a two-day journey by horse). The original Academy Building had no student accommodations until a twelve-room dormitory wing was added in 1810, and even then, the school did not fully meet the demand for student housing. Most students from out of town therefore had to live with families in private houses throughout the village.

During the second half of the nineteenth century, as the population of Deerfield and surrounding rural towns declined with the shift toward industry, enrollment dropped. The school also faced competition as other New England towns

Hinsdale and Anna Williams House, reconstructed boarder's room

opened their own public schools, thus reducing the need to send their children away for an education. In 1858, Deerfield Academy merged with the town's own newly founded public school—later known as the Dickinson High School—and by the end of the century it had become a purely local institution with a total student body of only about a dozen. (See Walk One, page 33.)

In 1902, however, Frank Boyden assumed leadership of the school and began the process of transforming it into the prestigious independent boarding school it is today, one that attracts students from across the country and around the world. Given the condition of the school he inherited, his ambition was extraordinary: he envisioned a fully residential institution that would provide for its students not just an education but also a home.

What physical form, though, should such an institution take? From an architectural standpoint, there were certainly precedents to consult. Deerfield's peer boarding schools primarily followed the model of the college campus, a self-contained and self-sufficient network of academic buildings supplemented by buildings for living: dining halls, athletics facilities, and of course, dormitories.

John Williams House

John Williams House, door detail

Boyden likewise aspired to this model, but he saw his school as unique. He felt that the Academy's role was to produce not just successful college students but citizens of strong character with a sense of loyalty to their community. He was enchanted by the village of Deerfield, which unlike many American towns had managed to successfully preserve its intimate scale and communal agrarian character, embodied in its exquisite stock of eighteenth-century houses. He saw in this close-knit and palpably ancient village an ideal model for the sort of community he wanted his students to create, and so he made every attempt to weave the Academy seamlessly into the town.

More than any other aspect of the campus, the development of the school's dormitory architecture has been defined by this effort to engage with and extend the village's unique sense of community and place. Even as the total number of students has grown to more than six hundred, the dormitories have always served to create smaller communities on the scale of a family. In addition to being durable and functional, these buildings provide a homelike environment for students as young as thirteen, most of whom are living away from their families for the first time. Indeed, one aspect that sets these dormitories apart from the college equivalent is the requirement that they include apartments for the faculty families responsible for looking after the boarding students. For Boyden's architects and their successors, a recurring design question was the extent to which dormitories, beyond functioning like large houses, ought also to look like houses—in particular, like the old houses that surround the campus. As we will see, different architects over the past century have taken various approaches to the design of Deerfield's dormitories, but all have responded in one way or another to the high bar set by the town's historic domestic architecture.

21 John Williams House

Builder unknown, 1760; addition, architect unknown, 1916; addition, Architectural Resources Cambridge, 2002

Bringing boarding students back to Deerfield was not originally Boyden's idea. That inspiration first came from one of Boyden's early students, Tom Ashley (class of 1911), whose story is among the Academy's most cherished legends. Ashley was a hopelessly introverted local boy, interested primarily in tramping around the woods by himself, shooting at local fauna. Boyden managed to cajole him into enrolling in the Academy in 1907 by inviting him to join in football games. Thanks to the headmaster's influence, Ashley grew into a successful student and athlete. On graduation, he attended Amherst College (Boyden's own alma mater), where he was a history major and a star player on the basketball, football, and baseball teams. He corresponded regularly with his former headmaster, and immediately after college, in 1916, he returned to Deerfield, where he taught history.

Ashley's devotion to Deerfield rivaled Boyden's. He spent his spare time sketching plans for the campus and drafting promotional material for the school.

Indeed, he provided Boyden with much of the early vision for the school's potential, insisting that Deerfield needed to grow, by once again enrolling students from out of town and housing them on campus. It was his enthusiasm that propelled the restoration and expansion of the eighteenth-century John Williams House on Albany Road as a dormitory and dining hall for several dozen students. This house was a fitting choice, considering that Deerfield's earliest boarding students lived with local families in their houses. In the fall of 1916, a group of students moved into the modest new ell appended to the back of John Williams House, and Deerfield once again became a boarding institution. Ashley served as their dormitory master until April of 1917, when the United States' entry into the First World War prompted him to enlist in the Marine Corps.

Ashley was killed in action the following year at the Battle of Belleau Wood. Despite his tragically brief tenure at Deerfield, his tireless dedication to the school has served as an inspiration for students and faculty ever since. For more than a century, Deerfield's headmasters and heads of school have exhorted students by reminding them of Ashley's belief that "if the spirit of Deerfield Academy could be condensed into a word, that word would be loyalty."

John Williams House itself has a notable history predating its role as an Academy dormitory. Over the years, there has been some debate as to its date of construction. In 1916, when it was converted to a dormitory, local tradition held that the house had been constructed by the town in 1707 as the residence for its famous minister, Reverend John Williams. Williams arrived in Deerfield in 1686 to oversee the spiritual needs of what was then a struggling frontier outpost. He was twenty-one years old when he took up the post—just a couple of years younger than Boyden was when he arrived to lead Deerfield Academy two centuries later. During the infamous French and Indian raid of 1704 (discussed further in Walk Five, pages 169 and 174), Williams's wife and two of his children were killed, and he was captured and marched to Canada with more than a hundred other townspeople. The French released Williams two years later, and on his return from Canada, the town of Deerfield built him a new house, where he lived until his death in 1729. It was this house that Ashley believed he was living in during his six months as a dormitory master. Subsequent study, however, has revealed that the 1707 house was in fact dismantled in 1760, when Williams's son Elijah replaced it with the present structure. This house originally stood farther to the east, right on the edge of the Town Common, but it was moved to its present site to make way for the construction of the Dickinson High School building in 1877.

The original 1760 front door of John Williams House is one of the finest examples of a Connecticut River Valley doorway. This door type was popular in Massachusetts and Connecticut towns throughout the valley around the middle of the eighteenth century. It is a quintessentially Georgian composition: the doors themselves are constructed of heavy raised panels arranged in various geometric configurations, sometimes with a row of small glass panes at the top of each leaf. The classical wood surround is usually composed of flanking pilasters set on

Cottonwood tree

pedestals and supporting an entablature with a broken scrolled pediment. At John Williams House, square blocks carved with elegant rosettes are placed between the pilaster capitals and the entablature in lieu of more elaborate, traditional capitals.

The Academy adopted this door in the 1920s as the principal icon of the Academy and the centerpiece of the school seal. In addition to recalling the historical and geographic context of the school, this distinctive architectural feature serves elegantly as a symbol of welcome and a metaphor for the opportunities opened through education.

In 2000, the Academy commissioned a specialty millwork shop, Architectural Components, to craft a highly accurate replica that would replace the original door, which is now preserved and on display at Historic Deerfield's Flynt Center for Early American Life.

22 Cottonwood Tree

Immediately to the north of John Williams House stood one of the largest trees in Deerfield. It was a cottonwood tree (*Populus deltoides*), one of several species that

Boyden Hall

thrive in New England's river valleys. The immense stature of this specimen was enhanced by its solitary position on the Quad, where it dwarfed the adjacent dormitory. Sadly, because of internal rot and deteriorating stability of the tree's core, the cottonwood was cut down in the summer of 2019.

23 Early Dormitories

a. Boyden Hall (a.k.a. Old Dorm), M. R. Drew, 1920; demolished, 1958
b. Plunkett Dormitory (a.k.a. New Dorm), Frank Irving Cooper, 1926; demolished, 1989

In 1920, Boyden oversaw the construction of a new dormitory, dramatically increasing the school's boarding capacity. Boyden Hall, as it came to be known, was the Academy's first new building since the completion of the Dickinson High School more than forty years earlier. The fact that Deerfield had grown large enough to necessitate a new dormitory was remarkable, given the diminished state of the school that Boyden had inherited, and in its architecture we can see his emerging ambitions for the school. In light of what would soon follow, it was a modest structure, tucked quietly behind John Williams House and barely visible from the main street. Compared with what Boyden had built to date, however, the dormitory projected a new confidence: it was its own building, not merely a shed tacked on to the back of an existing house.

Plunkett Dormitory

The architect of Boyden Hall, M. R. Drew of Greenfield, had recently worked on an addition for the Old Deerfield Arms Hotel (now the site of Pocumtuck Dormitory). For the dormitory, Drew employed a simple Colonial Revival style, compatible with the surrounding eighteenth-century houses, yet he gave it a more formal composition with a symmetrical H-shaped plan. The main entrance was at the center, facing south onto Albany Road and flanked by projecting gable ends of the east and west wings. A strong classical entablature unified the entire building, with the gables fully articulated as classical pediments. Drew counterbalanced this formality by using domestic-scaled details, such as a delicate entrance portico, double-hung windows with six panes per sash, dormers, and unpainted cedar shingle siding.

The ground floor of the west wing was devoted entirely to a spacious common room, designed to appear very much like the living room of a large house, complete with furniture arranged around a fireplace and with enough room for the entire student body to assemble (albeit sitting on the floor). This communal space was the embodiment of Boyden's philosophy: to create a tightly knit community, all of his students should be gathered together in one room on a daily basis. This is a tradition that continues to this day in the form of daily sit-down meals in the Dining Hall. Although Boyden Hall was demolished in 1958, the idea of the all-embracing common room remained central to the campus, and several very similar rooms were incorporated into subsequent buildings, including Plunkett Dormitory and the Main School Building.

Deerfield continued to expand after the completion of Boyden Hall, and in 1926 Charles Plunkett, then president of the board of trustees, contributed $50,000 for the construction of another dormitory. Plunkett selected as architect for the project Frank Irving Cooper of Boston, who two years earlier had renovated and expanded Ephraim Williams House as a home for the Boydens. Known for his experience with school buildings, Cooper had trained as a draftsman in the office of H. H. Richardson, a renowned nineteenth-century architect whose brilliantly idiosyncratic revival of the medieval Romanesque style came to be known as Richardsonian Romanesque. (His most famous design is the 1877 Trinity Church in Boston.) The influence of Richardson's characteristic style was evident in some of Cooper's designs, such as the 1894 Bristol County Superior Courthouse in his hometown of Taunton, Massachusetts, causing some to question Cooper's ability to design Colonial Revival buildings appropriate to Deerfield. Plunkett Dormitory, however, turned out to be an admirable essay in Colonial Revival style.

Plunkett was larger than Boyden Hall, more visible from the main street, and grander in its architectural expression. Housing sixty-six students, its plan was a *U* (rather than the *H* of Boyden Hall), with a broad eleven-bay facade facing Albany Road and forming the backdrop to a generous lawn. The central five bays were grouped together under a double-height portico supported by square Tuscan columns, above which perched three small pedimented dormers, a composition derived from the east facade of George Washington's house, Mount Vernon.

Cooper adapted the detailing primarily from local eighteenth-century precedents, and he tempered the rather grand allusion to Mount Vernon by using simple materials and details that allowed the building to sit comfortably amid the Yankee modesty of Deerfield's old houses. He clad the building in clapboards, for example, and for the front door he borrowed elements from the already iconic door of nearby John Williams House. In this way, Plunkett served as something of a stylistic bridge between the houses of old Deerfield and the grander academic buildings that would follow in subsequent decades.

Plunkett was demolished in 1989 to make way for Rosenwald-Shumway Dormitory.

24 Three Italianate Houses

a. Bewkes House (originally known as the Hoyt House), builder unknown, 1858; renovated by Deerfield Academy, 1926 (known as Chapin Dormitory); moved and renovated, 1951, 1998
b. Haynes House (originally the Orthodox Parsonage), builder unknown, 1849; moved and renovated by Deerfield Academy, 1952
c. Ashley House, builder unknown, 1869; renovated by Deerfield Academy, 1945; demolished, 2012

The town of Deerfield today is best known for its impressive stock of houses dating from about 1730 to 1830. This was a period of growth and prosperity for many

Haynes House

farming communities in New England, and it was characterized architecturally by the Georgian and Federal styles. After this period, New England's economy shifted toward industry, and Deerfield was rapidly eclipsed by nearby mill towns, such as Greenfield. This economic decline had the effect of preserving most of Deerfield's old farmhouses, which otherwise might have been demolished to make way for larger-scale development or more up-to-date houses. However, a handful of houses were built in Deerfield during the Victorian period, including one superb example of Carpenter Gothic (the Moors House, restored by Historic Deerfield) and several Italianate houses, including three owned by Deerfield Academy.

The most architecturally significant of these Italianate houses is currently known as Bewkes House. Bewkes was constructed for Arthur Hoyt in 1858 on the site of present-day Scaife Dormitory, directly opposite the Main School Building. The Hoyt family had a long history in Deerfield, first settling there around 1680. Arthur's father, Epaphras, was born in the Old Indian House in 1765 and was a leader in the town until his death in 1850. (See Walk Four, page 174.) Arthur, the only son of Epaphras and his wife, Experience, was educated by his father, a surveyor by trade. Arthur became a successful civil engineer, building railroads, roads, and canals and investing in mines and new towns across the Midwest.

Bewkes House

Befitting a prosperous engineer and investor, Hoyt's new house, which replaced an early colonial house of about 1706, was large and fashionable. On completion, it was assessed as the most valuable house in town. Over the following decades, the house changed hands a dozen times, until finally the Academy purchased it in 1926 and renovated it as a faculty and student residence known as Chapin Dormitory.

In 1951, to make way for the construction of Scaife Dormitory, Chapin was moved east to a new site, set back from the street, and rotated ninety degrees so that it was facing south toward Academy Lane (which runs eastward from the Common). It was moved again in 1998 to the other side of Academy Lane, now facing north, and again renamed, this time to Bewkes House. The ell was replaced and the main portion of the house was extensively remodeled to provide a faculty apartment on the second floor and administrative offices on the first floor. The house has since been returned to use as a dormitory, after further renovations by Thomas Douglas Architects of Northampton.

Bewkes exhibits many of the hallmarks of the Italianate style, which was popular in the United States from the 1850s to the 1860s, taking its inspiration from Italian Renaissance architecture. The nearly flat, hipped roof with deeply projecting eaves is meant to evoke the villas of Tuscany, where these features are well suited to the hot, dry climate (though it is fair to question the wisdom of adopting this roof form in New England). Furthermore, Bewkes forgoes the traditional New England clapboards in favor of flush boards, which emulate the smooth stucco finish of Italy's masonry construction. Arched windows are another typical characteristic of masonry architecture, and Bewkes features several of these in its projecting first-floor bays. Other windows are capped with pediments or flat cornices on brackets, both derived from Italian Renaissance sources. Lastly, like many Italianate houses, Bewkes has luxuriously tall first-floor windows shaded by open porches. The porches feature pairs of slender square columns supporting a gracefully arched entablature, with deep eaves echoing the main roof.

Although Bewkes is the grandest Italianate house in Deerfield, it was not the first. Its neighbor to the north, now known as Haynes House, had preceded it by almost a decade. Haynes was built in 1849 as the parsonage for the Orthodox Congregational Church (also known as the White Church) on Memorial Street, which had broken off from the First Congregational Church (the Brick Church) when the congregation of the latter converted to Unitarianism in 1835.

Whereas the architectural style of the White Church is Greek Revival, its parsonage of a decade later is decidedly Italianate. Though humbler than Bewkes, Haynes has several similar features, including flush-board siding, tall first-floor windows, and a low hipped roof, but with eaves supported by paired brackets. The entrance is marked by a quirky porch supported by somewhat squat Corinthian columns on pedestals. In a close parallel with Bewkes, Haynes was removed from its prominent site on the Street in 1952 to make way for Mather Dormitory. It now

Ashley House, photograph from 1945

serves as a faculty residence and occupies a site at the end of Academy Lane, not far from where its original neighbor ended up in 1998.

The last of the Academy's Italianate houses, Ashley House, was built at the far northern end of the Street in 1869. Its original owner, Jonathan Ashley, had grown up on his family's ancestral homestead, which had been built by his namesake, Reverend Jonathan Ashley, in 1734. (See Walk Four, page 162). After living in the old house for many years, the younger Jonathan had it moved to the back of his lot and repurposed as a barn. He built a new house "of modern style" in its place.

Though this house had a front-facing pediment rather than a low hipped roof, many of its other details were nearly identical to those of Bewkes, including the window surrounds, the small arched windows (here in the gable), and the porch, with its delicate square columns and slightly arched entablature.

In 1945, when pioneering preservationists Henry and Helen Flynt (discussed in Walk Four, page 159) began restoration on the older Jonathan Ashley House, Deerfield Academy purchased the 1869 Jonathan Ashley House, moved it to Academy Lane, and renovated it as a dormitory. It was soon joined by Haynes and then Bewkes, and it remained there until 2012, when the Academy demolished it to make way for a new dormitory.

The parallels between these three houses are striking, and they serve as a powerful illustration of the shifts in architectural fashion over time. All three were built on prominent lots on the Street where they replaced older houses of the colonial period, which at that time were considered outdated. All three suffered a reversal of fortune a century later, when they themselves came to be seen as stylistically irrelevant amid a renewed interest in colonial history and architecture. And as a result, all three were removed to the same inconspicuous side street and replaced by structures of a style almost identical to that of the colonial houses they themselves had originally replaced. Today, their legacy is mixed: Haynes has been generally overlooked, Bewkes renovated at great expense, and Ashley demolished.

25 Midcentury Colonial Revival Dormitories

a. Scaife Dormitory, William & Geoffrey Platt, 1952
b. Mather Dormitory, William & Geoffrey Platt, 1953
c. Pocumtuck Dormitory, Williams & Geoffrey Platt, 1956;
addition, Architectural Resources Cambridge, 1999
d. Field Dormitory, William & Geoffrey Platt, 1957
e. McAlister Dormitory, William & Geoffrey Platt, 1958

Between 1952 and 1958, William and Geoffrey Platt oversaw the construction of five Colonial Revival dormitories, fulfilling a design concept first sketched out by Charles Platt in the 1930s. The five buildings conform to identical plans while varying in their details. Mather, Scaife, and Pocumtuck stand in a row along the Street directly across from the Main School Building; McAlister and Field are located at the western end of Albany Road, next to the Old Burying Ground.

Scaife Dormitory, door detail

Pocumtuck Dormitory, door detail

These were the first new dormitories to be built since Boyden and Plunkett Dormitories in the 1920s, and in contrast to those early dorms, this new set was defined by the radical idea that dorms should look like houses rather than institutional buildings. The Platts designed them to complete the eighteenth-century imagery of the Street, replacing stylistic outliers of the Victorian period, like Haynes and Bewkes, with buildings that evoked the town's earlier history. Fundraising literature for their construction highlights the architecture's fidelity to eighteenth-century models, referring to them as "colonial replica dormitories" and emphasizing that they were to be "a part of colonial Deerfield."

Indeed, these dormitories were remarkable for their attention to historical detail and craftsmanship; for instance, they were originally built with authentically detailed divided-light windows and operable wood shutters. Although the Academy has discarded these features in recent renovations, other details remain. Of particular note are the front door surrounds, which are all different but all derived from historical examples found along the Street. These are not slavish replicas; rather, the Platts carefully studied and then reinterpreted—and in some ways refined—local design sources. The front door surround of Scaife, for example, combines elements from those of the Manse and the Joseph Stebbins House but renders the details in a more classically correct fashion. The door surround of Pocumtuck takes that of the 1755 Sheldon House as a starting point, adding a transom window and adjusting the moldings. (See Walk Four, pages 149, 152, and 161.)

OVERLEAF **Mather and Scaife Dormitories**

68

Barton Dormitory

While the historical details are used to connect these buildings to their older neighbors, they also serve to differentiate the five dormitories from each other. Though conforming to nearly identical plans, their design skillfully avoids monotony. Window and door details vary; roofs alternate between simple pitches and gambrels; and each house adopts a different color scheme. Even subtleties like the number of chimneys or the spacing of the windows are manipulated to create variety within the ensemble.

26 Barton Dormitory

William & Geoffrey Platt, 1962

Barton Dormitory is named after Academy trustee Bruce Barton, a successful publicist, magazine editor, advertising executive, and US congressman from New York from 1937 to 1940. For fifty years, he devoted his advertising talent to helping Boyden promote Deerfield's cause.

In 1929, Barton produced a plush, limited-edition book about the Academy, which served as the cornerstone of a fundraising campaign that over the next decade would enable the construction of the school's most prominent buildings. This book included perhaps the first statement of what would become the school's motto, "Be worthy of your heritage," as well as one of the first uses of the John Williams House door, printed in green ink, as an icon for the school. These would soon become the dominant elements of the school seal.

Barton served on the board of trustees from 1956 to 1967, and in 1962, along with Helen and Frank Boyden, he was an inaugural recipient of the Deerfield Medal for distinguished service to the Academy. Barton Dormitory was dedicated the same year.

Considering the preceding series of house-like dormitories built in the 1950s, the design for Barton comes as something of a surprise: it is the first Deerfield dormitory to be constructed entirely of brick and marks a return to the institutional formality of Plunkett. William and Geoffrey Platt were once again the architects, and the size and floor plan are nearly identical to their five previous dormitories—so why the sudden shift in style?

The site suggests an answer: Barton sits at the west end of Albany Road, across from the Field Dormitory. Like the five house-type dormitories, its narrow end faces the street, and the scale of that facade does have a rather domestic quality. Unlike the other dormitories, however, Barton's long flank plays an important role: it provides the western architectural backdrop to the Academy's central Quad and responds visually to the Main School Building at the opposite end of the Quad. This accounts for the use of brick and the symmetrical Palladian/Georgian composition of the long facade, which consists of a two-and-a-half-story central block with gambrel roof and dormers connected by hyphens to projecting end pavilions with hipped roofs. The twin entrances on Barton's east facade also mirror those on the west facade of the Main School Building. Though Barton's design was unusual in the context of the previous dorms, it set an important precedent for those that would follow over the next several decades.

27 Dormitory Quadrangles

a. Johnson and Doubleday Dormitories,
Timothy D. Smith & Associates, 1981
b. Rosenwald-Shumway Dormitory,
Edward Larrabee Barnes Associates, 1989
c. DeNunzio Dormitory, Edward Larrabee Barnes Associates, 1989
d. John Louis Dormitory, David Childs (Skidmore, Owings & Merrill) with Architectural Resources Cambridge, 1998
e. Louis Marx Dormitory, David Childs (Skidmore, Owings & Merrill) with Architectural Resources Cambridge, 1998

During the whole of Boyden's tenure as headmaster, from the beginning of the twentieth century through the 1960s, Deerfield had consistently lined up its dormitories along the Street and Albany Road, just as if they were ordinary houses. Starting in

McAllister and Field Dormitories

Johnson and Doubleday Dormitories

the 1980s, however, the Academy's architects began to conceive of new dorms as opportunities to create quadrangles, thereby giving an enhanced spatial organization to the campus and providing outdoor communal spaces. The following three pairs of dormitories demonstrate the approaches taken by three different architects to this type of design.

Johnson and Doubleday, designed by the Vermont-based firm Timothy Smith & Associates in 1981, are the first of this new generation of dormitories. The two buildings are identical twins, hyphenated by a large common room known as Crow Commons after Robert Crow, a longtime member of the history department and head of the alumni office. With a hundred beds combined, Johnson and Doubleday make up Deerfield's largest dormitory complex to date—they house all of the ninth-grade students—yet their defining architectural characteristic is their modesty. The buildings seem embarrassed by their size, as if they are attempting to minimize their presence on campus. Tucked inconspicuously behind the Manse, they are stacked, one behind the other, so that the full bulk of the complex is hidden as one approaches from the Street.

Unlike the previous generation of dorms, Johnson and Doubleday are not long and straight; they curl up to form two small identical courtyards, each with a narrow

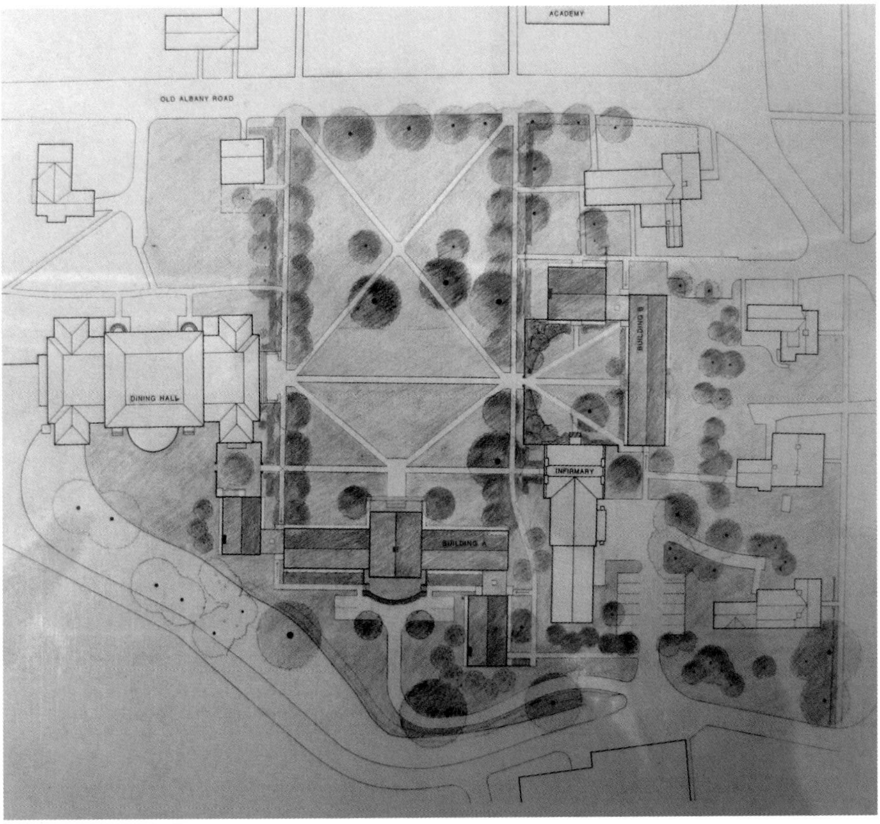

Plan of Rosenwald-Shumway and DeNunzio Dormitories

opening at the southeast corner. The buildings are arranged such that the north and west ranges of each quadrangle are two and a half stories, while the south and east ranges are lower to admit more sunlight. This varied massing disguises the full scale of the complex, making it seem like a collection of many smaller buildings, especially from the south, which is the most prominent view. This reading is reinforced by the use of different materials for different wings. Some are brick, while others have wood clapboards.

The architectural style is as self-effacing as the overall massing. Forgoing the elegant Colonial Revival features that were the hallmark of every previous dorm, Johnson and Doubleday opt for an abstracted vernacular idiom. Some of the forms recall barns and outbuildings, while the brick portions allude vaguely to the more formal neo-Georgian architecture of Barton. Regrettably, though, the potential charm of this varied assemblage is thwarted by its consistently bland detailing.

Johnson and Doubleday were followed eight years later by another pair of dorms: Rosenwald-Shumway and DeNunzio. Rosenwald was made possible by a gift from John (class of 1948) and Pat Rosenwald, and Shumway by a gift from Forrest (class of 1945) and Patsy Shumway. Former Academy trustee Ralph DeNunzio and his wife, Jean, gave the gift to build DeNunzio in honor of their three sons, who attended Deerfield.

Dewey House (left) and Rosenwald-Shumway Dormitory (right)

To design the new dorms, the Academy selected architect Edward Larrabee Barnes, whose highly regarded firm had designed numerous academic and cultural projects throughout the country. Unlike the introverted Johnson-Doubleday, this new pair takes up a highly visible location and engages with several prominent existing buildings. It also replaces Plunkett Dormitory, a venerable structure that had occupied the site since 1926.

The demolition of Plunkett—as well as the Barn, which had been used for everything from athletics practices to Glee Club performances—opened up a large swath of land between the Dining Hall and the Health Center (now Dewey). Rather than reoccupying this space, however, Barnes deployed the new dorms around the periphery, linking the two older buildings together to define a new quadrangle. To do this, he pushed the facade of Rosenwald-Shumway back as far as possible to the south, while maintaining a strong axial alignment with the Memorial Building across the Quad to the north. This allowed the Dining Hall entrance facade, which had once faced the unceremonious flank of Plunkett, to open onto the newly created space.

To center this space and give it a sense of clarity, though, Barnes needed to create a strong east-west cross-axis, aligned with the Dining Hall entrance. Here he was faced with a problem: Even though Dewey and the Dining Hall had both been designed at the same time and by the same architect, the massive presence of Plunkett standing between them had precluded any thought of giving the two buildings a strong geometric relationship with one another. (See Walk Two, pages 75 and 78.) As a result, the main entrance to Dewey is offset from that of the Dining Hall and at right angles to it, facing instead toward Albany Road. Barnes solved this challenge in an ingenious way: He began by placing the main entrance to DeNunzio directly opposite that of the Dining Hall, but set back from the perpendicular facade of Dewey. With the cross-axis thus established, he reinforced it further by mirroring the primary mass of Dewey, giving DeNunzio its prominent northern wing. The resulting building is L-shaped. Although asymmetrical on its own, together with Dewey it creates a symmetrical forecourt directly across from the Dining Hall. This is campus planning at its best: new buildings designed not as isolated showpieces, but as team players, enhancing the existing built fabric to create a dynamic and harmonious ensemble.

In light of the masterly plan governing the layout of Rosenwald-Shumway and DeNunzio, the architecture itself comes as a disappointment. The scale, composition, and materials are generally in line with the surrounding brick Georgian buildings designed by the Platts from the 1930s through the 1950s. Rosenwald-Shumway, for example, features the classically Palladian composition of a pedimented central pavilion flanked by symmetrical wings. This is the same compositional strategy found in the Main School Building, Arms Building, Memorial Building, and others, yet Barnes's detailing suffers by comparison. Moldings are absent, and the only features that might be considered ornamental are the brick soldier courses (rows of bricks standing on end), one located at the base (or water table) and another just beneath the rather feeble wood cornice. Windows, doors, and other traditionally celebrated architectural features are treated here as merely utilitarian.

OPPOSITE **DeNunzio Dormitory and Dewey House**

John Louis Dormitory

John Louis Dormitory, interior

The Academy made some effort to remedy this problem in the late 1990s when it replaced many of the original single-pane (and barely functional) awning windows with traditional double-hung windows of eight- and twelve-pane sashes. This addressed the windows of the dormitory rooms only, not the common rooms, leaving an unsatisfactory mixture of traditional and minimalist window treatments.

David Childs (class of 1959), of Skidmore, Owings & Merrill, designed the last of the three pairs of dormitories, John Louis and Louis Marx, which were completed in 1998. This was the second of three major projects that Childs executed at Deerfield, the first being the Natatorium and the third the Koch Center. The site was an amorphous and somewhat neglected area at the east end of campus, behind Mather and Scaife dorms and next to Johnson and Doubleday. But where Johnson and Doubleday seem to hide in the background, John Louis and Louis Marx are architectural extroverts. Like Barnes, Childs designed his dorms as highly "social" buildings that reach out and forge connections with existing buildings, establishing new spatial relationships between previously disconnected parts of the campus.

Louis Marx Dormitory

It is clear that Childs studied the Barnes dorms closely, as he employed a number of similar planning techniques. His two dorms work with each other and with existing buildings to shape a large new quadrangle. Like Barnes, Childs uses bilateral symmetry to organize the design but sacrifices the symmetry of the individual building where necessary in order to create a more harmonious relationship with the rest of the ensemble. Just as the centralized facade of Rosenwald-Shumway responds to the axis of the Memorial Building at the opposite end of the Quad, John Louis responds to the axis of the Main School Building on the other side of the Street. However, the path of this axis is not as clear a shot; it crosses the street and threads between Mather and Scaife before reaching the main entrance of John Louis, so a more conspicuous marker is required as a visual beacon: only a tower will do!

The John Louis tower is square in plan, a brick shaft crowned by a tall band of windows, a steeply pitched pediment, and a spire-like cupola set at forty-five degrees to the ridge. The tower communicates with the Main School Building not only through space but also through time: its geometry refers explicitly to the tower of the 1877 Dickinson High School building, which had been demolished to make way

Louis Marx Dormitory, interior

for the current Main School Building in 1930. (See Walk One, page 33.) Whereas the older tower had been placed off-center, part of a picturesque Victorian composition, the later reincarnation confidently asserts the center of its strongly axial dormitory, marking the main entrance and central common room. Also in contrast to the older version, the interior of this tower is uninterrupted by stairs or floors, resulting in a dramatic vertical shaft of space.

Like Barnes's DeNunzio, the L-shaped Louis Marx plays a supporting role in the ensemble. Its asymmetrical placement to the south of John Louis's central axis serves as a counterbalance to Johnson and Doubleday to the north. In a harmonious counterpoint to the erect tower of John Louis, the central entrance to Louis Marx is marked by a two-story core that is oval in plan. This geometry functions elegantly as a pivot between the two perpendicular wings and generates a striking second-floor common room that is lit by an elliptical halo of clerestory windows.

By working together and even drawing in the reluctant Johnson and Doubleday buildings, the Childs dorms form a dynamic yet balanced quadrangle, anchoring a newly assertive eastern side of the campus. Moreover, their detailing is of a much higher quality than either of the two preceding sets of dorms. Like Barnes, Childs uses brick for his dormitories, but he goes much further in exploring the ornamental possibilities of the material, employing a variety of colors and bond patterns, ornamental stringcourses between floors, and arches (both round and flat) for the window and door openings. In this regard, he surpasses even the work of the Platts. The woodwork is somewhat less skillfully handled, especially in comparison with the work of the first half of the twentieth century; however, it is a dramatic improvement over the dorm's immediate predecessors.

By combining these details and materials with the symmetrically composed facades, Childs set his dorms firmly within the Colonial/Georgian tradition that had defined the school from its founding through the 1960s. In this context, his creative site planning and inventive tower and oval are all the more striking. Perhaps more than any other building on campus, these dormitories demonstrate the potential for a single design to successfully harness the opposing forces of tradition and innovation. Here, rather than canceling each other out, they magnify each other.

28 Recent Colonial Revival Dormitories

a. Harold Webster Smith Dormitory, Architectural Resources Cambridge, 2002
b. O'Byrne Curtis Dormitory, Architectural Resources Cambridge, 2012

With the two most recently completed dormitories, the architectural pendulum swings once more toward the house model (as seen in the Midcentury Colonial Revival Dormitories). Both projects were designed by Architectural Resources Cambridge (ARC), a national firm that focuses on educational and corporate projects.

The first dormitory, Harold Webster Smith, was given to the Academy by Mr. and Mrs. Winthrop Smith Jr. (class of 1967), the Winthrop and Margaret Smith Family Foundation, Mrs. Harold Webster Smith, and Mr. and Mrs. James C. Smith (class of 1967) in honor of Harold Webster Smith (class of 1929). The building was constructed in 2002 on Albany Road, just west of John Williams House. This was the exact site that had been occupied by Boyden Hall from 1920 to 1958, but the layout of the new dormitory is much more closely aligned with the Platt dormitories of the 1950s (now with an even more explicitly barnlike wing on the back). This approach makes sense given that Harold Smith joins a small cluster of eighteenth-century houses, fitting right in with John Williams House, Hitchcock House, and the Little Brown House. The disadvantage is that Harold Smith faces Albany Road but doesn't simultaneously address the Quad behind it, as Boyden Hall had done.

Harold Smith is notable for the high quality of its architectural detailing, which is on par with the Colonial Revival dormitories of the 1950s. Like them, it is not a precise replica of any eighteenth-century house but is designed in the same style with great attention to detail. Especially satisfying is the robust and competently detailed front door surround, which is adapted from one built for the eighteenth-century Allen House when it was restored in the 1940s.

The second of the two ARC dormitories, completed in 2012, was until very recently still to be named; it was provisionally referred to as "New Dorm" for seven years. New Dorm was renamed O'Byrne Curtis in honor of retiring Head of School

Harold Webster Smith Dormitory

O'Byrne Curtis Dormitory

Margarita O'Byrne Curtis in May of 2019. It is located on the Academy Lane site previously occupied by Ashley House, which was demolished to make way for it. Although O'Byrne Curtis is stylistically related to Harold Smith, it is less like a house than a collage of house-like components. Its style is vaguely Colonial Revival, but without Harold Smith's careful detailing.

What O'Byrne Curtis may lack in architectural grace, it makes up for in ecological sustainability. Solar hot-water panels blanket the south-facing slope of the roof, and the building is lit entirely with high-efficiency LED fixtures. This

much-needed attention to the ecological impact of buildings will undoubtedly remain a central consideration for future design work at Deerfield. Perhaps the next dormitory will combine the environmental sustainability of O'Byrne Curtis with the aesthetic achievement of Harold Smith, the Childs dorms, and those of previous generations.

WALK FOUR

An Extraordinary Legacy: Notable Deerfield Residents and Their Houses

29 Ephraim Williams House
30 The Manse
31 Joseph Stebbins House
32 Hitchcock House
33 The Little Brown House
34 Allen House
35 Sheldon House
36 Ashley House

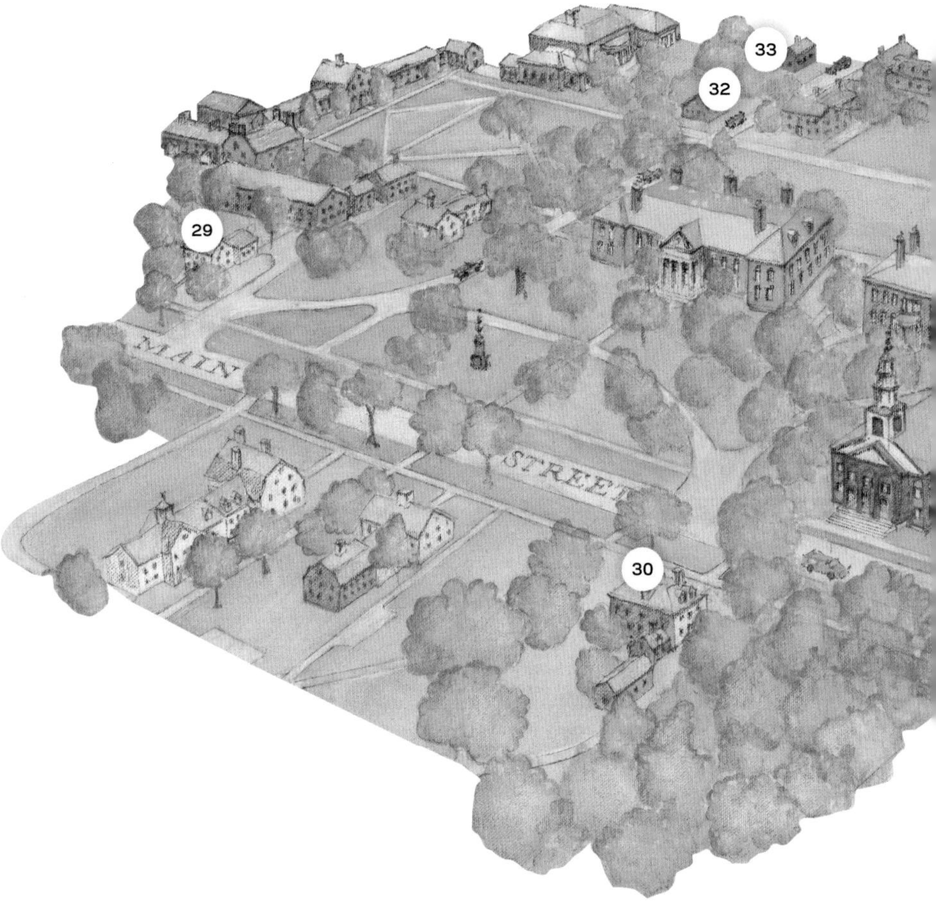

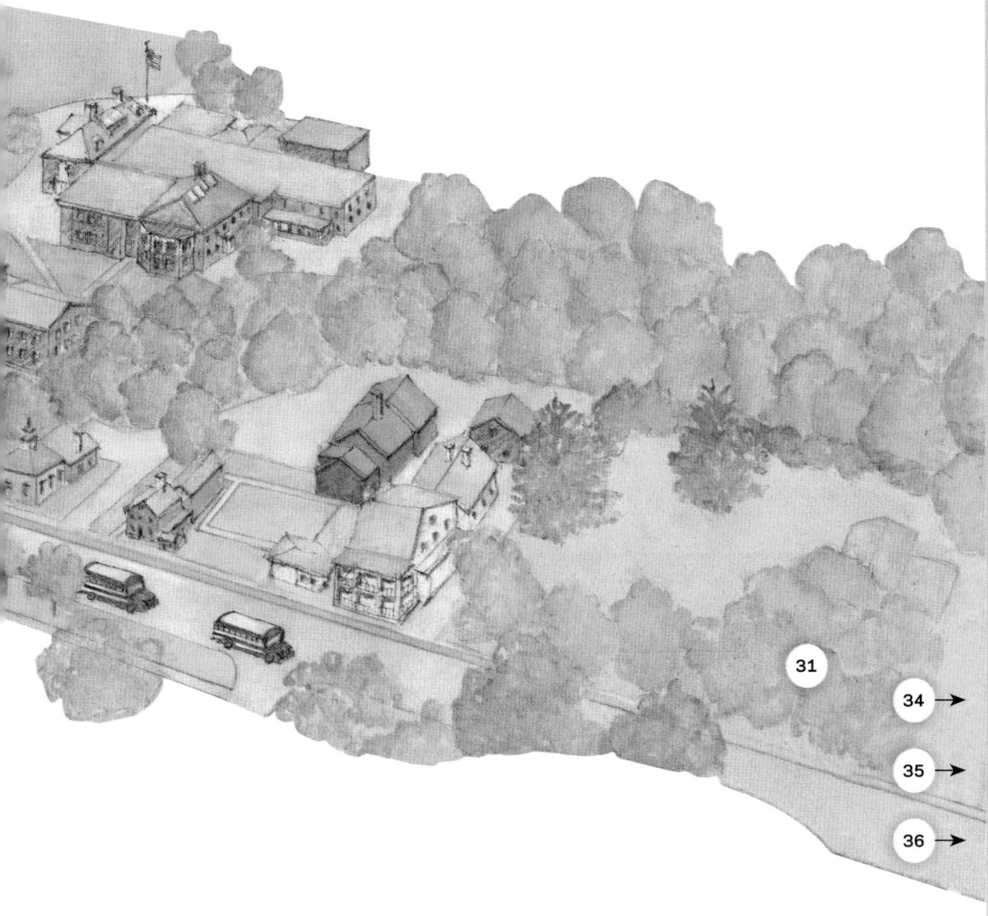
31
34
35
36

WALK FOUR

An Extraordinary Legacy: Notable Deerfield Residents and Their Houses

To anyone interested in the history of American architecture, Deerfield's mile-long Old Main Street (better known as "the Street") presents a spectacular gallery of more than forty well-preserved houses of the eighteenth and early nineteenth centuries. These houses offer not only unique architectural insights but also an opportunity to explore the lives of those who have inhabited them. In studying just a handful of these residents, one is inevitably struck by the extraordinary number of intellectuals who have made their home in this little farming village over the past three and a half centuries.

Some were ministers, such as John Williams, Jonathan Ashley, and Samuel Willard. Many pursued scientific studies, among them Edward and Orra White Hitchcock, Jennie Arms Sheldon, and Helen Childs Boyden. An even greater number were artists: the Fullers, the Allen sisters, Annie Putnam, and again, Orra White Hitchcock. Largest of all is the cohort of historians and preservationists, including George Sheldon, Samuel Willard, C. Alice Baker, Madeline Wynne, Annie Putnam, Henry and Helen Flynt, and William Gass. It was largely through their efforts that Deerfield retained so much of its bucolic and historical character, qualities that in turn inspired and informed Deerfield Academy's campus.

The great majority of these Deerfield residents were associated with the Academy in one way or another, whether as students, faculty members, trustees, or benefactors. In the following walk, we will touch on a few of these remarkable characters as well as the houses they lived in. We begin with several Academy-owned houses along Albany Road (with the notable omission of John Williams House, covered in Walk Three, page 109). We then head north along the Street, stopping at three museum houses owned by Historic Deerfield and regularly open to the public.

29 Ephraim Williams House

Builder unknown, ca. 1760; addition, Frank Irving Cooper, 1924; addition, Kuhn Riddle Architects, 2011

Ephraim Williams House sits at the intersection of the Street and Albany Road at the southern edge of the Town Common. The house has several connections to Colonel Ephraim Williams, a colonial soldier who was killed in the French and Indian Wars in 1755, leaving money in his will for the foundation of Williams College. Colonel Williams himself never lived in the house, however. It was built around 1760, several years after his death, for John Partridge Bull, a gunsmith and armorer for a regiment led by Colonel Israel Williams, Ephraim's cousin. The Williams family acquired the property in 1794, and by the turn of the twentieth century, the house was inhabited

Ephraim Williams House

Ephraim Williams House, interior

Ephraim Williams House, portico (demolished, 2011)

by a Captain Ephraim Williams, great-great-grand-nephew of the more famous colonel. It was this Captain Williams, a trustee of the Academy, who greeted Frank Boyden when he first arrived in Deerfield in August of 1902 to become the school's headmaster. (See Walk One, page 36.)

In 1924, the Academy purchased and renovated Ephraim Williams House to serve as an administrative center for the school and a residence for the Boydens. They lived there from 1926 until 1968, and during this period, the Boydens made the house not only their home but also a sort of living room for the entire school, frequently hosting students and faculty in their large, low-ceilinged parlor.

After retiring, the Boydens moved across the street to the Manse, and Ephraim Williams was repurposed to serve as a dormitory and faculty residence. In 1999, the house was retired from residential use and given over to the Academy's Office of Advancement, which has occupied it ever since. For a time, the back portion of the building also housed the Academy's bookstore. Today, the house retains many of its eighteenth-century interiors, and the refurbished "living room" in the west wing is beautifully appointed with early American antiques.

Architect Frank Irving Cooper, who was soon also to design Plunkett Dormitory next door, oversaw the 1924 renovation and addition to Ephraim Williams House. Similar to the work done on John Williams House in 1916, Cooper's strategy was to extend the existing ell westward, leaving the front of the house undisturbed. With this approach, he followed a long tradition in New England of adding on to the backs of houses (many examples can be found in Deerfield). Typically, these extended houses become increasingly utilitarian the farther back they go, often terminating in a barn for livestock. But Cooper knew that his addition was expanding not just away from the Street but also toward a future campus. Accordingly, he reversed the normal progression, such that the architecture of Ephraim Williams becomes even more formal at the new western end, where he added an elegant two-story portico. This consisted of four delicately proportioned Tuscan columns supporting a pediment with a half-round window. The square columns were similar in style to those he would soon employ for the broader portico of Plunkett.

In 2011, Kuhn Riddle Associates was hired to further expand the house in order to accommodate additional space for the Office of Advancement. They did this by filling in the portico, eliminating most of the entablature, and replacing the Tuscan columns with abstracted, postmodern pilasters.

30 The Manse

Builder unknown, 1769, with addition, ca. 1800; restored by Henry and Helen Flynt, 1950

The Manse, like Ephraim Williams House, has seen a number of noteworthy residents over the course of its 250-year history. The main portion of the house was constructed beginning in 1769 for Joseph Barnard. Among its early residents were two nineteenth-century preceptors of Deerfield Academy, Hosea Hildreth and Luther Lincoln.

Perhaps the most important early resident was the Reverend Samuel Willard, who purchased the house in 1811. Willard served as Deerfield's minister from 1807 to 1829 and was notable for bringing the liberal theology of Unitarianism to western Massachusetts. As a result, he was shunned by the more orthodox Congregational ministers of the Connecticut Valley. In Deerfield, however, his intelligence, generosity, and energy endeared him to many, and the town benefited from his leadership in numerous ways.

Willard devoted much time to the cause of education: Before coming to Deerfield, he had taught at both Philips Exeter Academy and Bowdoin College. He later served as president of Deerfield Academy's board of trustees for two decades as well as superintendent of the local public schools, for which he wrote several elementary-level primers. He was also an avid musician and worked to improve the quality of music at his church. He published several hymnals during his career, including the *Deerfield Collection of Sacred Music* in 1808.

Willard brought equal enthusiasm to the physical improvement and beautification of the town and organized the planting of hundreds of elms, sycamores, and maples along the Street. In 1823, he successfully advocated for the construction of a new meetinghouse, now known as the Brick Church. And in 1847, he spearheaded a regrettably unsuccessful campaign to preserve one of the oldest houses in town, the 1699 Old Indian House. (See Walk Five, page 174.) This effort is believed to have been the first organized architectural preservation campaign in the United States.

The Manse

In 1885, the Manse was purchased by two Boston women, Madeline Wynne and Annie Putnam. (See also the Little Brown House, page 158.) Wynne was heiress to the Yale lock fortune and an artist who, over her lifetime, explored a variety of media, including metalwork, painting, woodwork, basketry, and writing. Wynne left her husband, with whom she had two sons, in 1874. She met Putnam, a fellow craftswoman (and fellow heiress) while traveling in Italy in 1880. Putnam was a painter, potter, metalworker, and musician (a Deerfield neighbor remembers her once stringing together overturned flowerpots to play as an instrument at a gathering). The two women developed a lifelong relationship, spending winters in their Boston art studio and summers in Deerfield. In 1901, Wynne founded the Deerfield Society of Arts and Crafts—Putnam was an avid member—and the two were active leaders of Deerfield's vibrant arts community.

Upon purchase of the Willard House, Wynne and Putnam oversaw the first historically minded house restoration in Deerfield. As part of the renovation, they added a screened porch to the rear, as well as a portico to the side entrance on the south, reusing wood columns salvaged from the town's former meetinghouse of 1729. (These have since been removed and can now be found in the Memorial Hall Museum.) They renamed their renovated home the Manse.

Deerfield Academy purchased the Manse in 1928, and in 1950 it was restored again by Henry and Helen Flynt for use as an Academy guesthouse. (See the Allen House, page 159.) Frank and Helen Boyden moved into the house on their retirement in 1968, and since 1980 the Manse has served as the official residence of the Academy's heads of school—Robert Kaufmann, Eric Widmer, Margarita O'Byrne Curtis, and now John P. N. Austin.

The Manse is perhaps the handsomest house in Deerfield and occupies a prominent site on a slight rise just across the street from the Brick Church. The main block, built in 1769, exemplifies the Georgian style typical of late colonial architecture. A perfect square in plan, it is capped by a double-hipped roof with two dormers on each side. The corners are visually reinforced by wood quoins, an architectural representation of masonry blocks. The front door surround is a classical composition, with fluted pilasters supporting an entablature with a pulvinated (bulging) frieze and a segmental (curved) pediment. The interior is of equal architectural caliber, with raised paneling in many rooms and an elaborate staircase. The ell, which was added around the turn of the nineteenth century, incorporates reused timbers from a house built on the lot in the early eighteenth century.

31 Joseph Stebbins House

Builder unknown, 1773; renovated by Deerfield Academy, ca. 1952, 2012

The house just to the north of the Deerfield Inn was built in 1773 for Joseph Stebbins Jr., who would later become one of Deerfield Academy's founding trustees and early benefactors. The year that the Stebbins House was completed, Bostonians protesting royal taxation dumped a shipment of tea into Boston Harbor, pushing the

The Manse, front-door detail

Joseph Stebbins House

American colonies closer toward armed conflict with England. The Boston Tea Party and other events leading up to the American Revolution split colonists—including Deerfield's citizens—into two political camps: the loyal Tories and the rebellious Whigs. Whigs began to gain political strength in Deerfield in the early 1770s, and in 1774 they erected a liberty pole just across the street from the newly constructed Stebbins House.

In the following years, Joseph Stebbins Jr. proved to be one of the town's most avid Whigs (as later recorded by his historian grandson, George Sheldon). (See the Sheldon House, page 161.) On April 20, 1775, when news of the Battle of Lexington reached Deerfield, Stebbins was a lieutenant in the local company of minutemen, who rushed to Boston in response. On arrival, he was promoted to captain and several weeks later he commanded a company of men—including some from Deerfield—at the Battle of Bunker Hill. Stebbins fought in several engagements during the war, including the Battle of Saratoga, and eventually achieved the rank of colonel.

Despite Stebbins's revolutionary fervor, his house is the embodiment of the period's architectural establishment. It is one of the largest in Deerfield and shares many architectural features with the Manse, which had been constructed just four years earlier. Both have a square plan with four large rooms per floor in the main block and a broad central stair hall. The Stebbins front door surround is similar to that of the Manse: two pilasters supporting an entablature with a segmental pediment. It displays an even greater level of craftsmanship, though, following the more elaborate Ionic order, with its characteristic scrolled volutes in the column capitals, and arching each pane of glass in the transom window. The most notable difference

Hitchcock House

between the houses is in their roofs: whereas the Manse has an elegant double-hipped roof, the Stebbins House opts for a more conventional gambrel roof. Because of the depth of the house, the Stebbins gambrel is very large, allowing for two tiers of attic windows in the gables.

The house remained in the Stebbins family until 1898, when it was sold to Academy trustee Jennie Arms Sheldon. Deerfield Academy rented the house after Sheldon's death in 1938 and eventually purchased it in 1952, at which point the school renovated it for use as a faculty and student residence. The house underwent a second renovation by the Academy in 2012.

32 Hitchcock House

Builder unknown, 1779; dining hall addition, Kirkham & Parlett, ca. 1920; renovated as bookstore, 2001

Just west of Ephraim Williams House and across Albany Road from John Williams House, sits Hitchcock House, a compact red saltbox currently occupied by the Academy bookstore. The house was built for Justin Hitchcock in 1779, and his family lived there until 1900.

By far the most notable members of the Hitchcock family were Justin's youngest son, Edward, and his wife, Orra White Hitchcock. Justin, a hatter, could not afford an extensive education for his children, and Edward's only formal schooling consisted of six winter terms at Deerfield Academy. Nonetheless, he had a strong intellectual curiosity and pursued an early interest in astronomy and other sciences.

He would later recall that "the great comet of 1811, and access to some good instruments for observing it, belonging to Deerfield Academy, gave me a decided bias for astronomy." Although Hitchcock lacked any college education, the Academy trustees recognized his scholarly aptitude, and in 1816, they appointed him preceptor, a post he held until 1818. The Academy's preceptress during the same years was Orra White, who was from South Amherst, and the two were married in 1821.

Edward left Deerfield to study theology and science at Yale. After serving for several years as minister of the Congregational Church in Conway, Massachusetts, he returned to academia as professor of chemistry and natural history at Amherst College, which had been founded only a few years earlier. In 1845, Edward became president of Amherst College, a position he held until 1854. He continued to teach geology and natural theology there until his death in 1864.

Edward's wide-ranging academic interests are reflected in his numerous published works. His first publication was an annual *Country Almanac*, printed from 1814 to 1818, which he advertised as being "adapted to the convenience of farmers... containing more than an ordinary number of astronomical calculations, and other matters instructive, useful, and entertaining." Subsequent titles include *Lectures on the Peculiar Phenomena of the Four Seasons* (1850), *The Religion of Geology and Its Connected Sciences* (1851), and *Dyspepsia Forestalled and Resisted: Or, Lectures on Diet, Regimen, and Employment* (1830). His most significant work, however, was the nearly seven-hundred-page *Report on the Geology, Mineralogy, Botany, and Zoology of Massachusetts*, which was commissioned by the state government, published in 1833, and reprinted three times.

Two geographic features that he studied were later named in his honor: Mount Hitchcock is a peak in the Holyoke Range, just south of Amherst, and Lake Hitchcock is a prehistoric body of water that once occupied much of what is now the Connecticut River Valley.

Orra was an equally noteworthy academic. As preceptress of Deerfield Academy, she taught fine and decorative arts, mathematics, botany, and astronomy, and she organized the Young Ladies Literary Society. In 1818, she returned to her hometown to serve as preceptress at Amherst Academy, the precursor to Amherst College.

After her marriage to Edward, she devoted much of her efforts to the production of hundreds of drawings, engravings, and watercolors illustrating his publications. Her *Herbarium Parvum Pictum*, for example, a portfolio assembled between 1817 and 1821, contains dozens of watercolors of botanical specimens, all meticulously detailed, highly accurate, and beautifully rendered. Orra also produced illustrations of local landscapes, geologic formations, fossils, and hundreds of large classroom charts to aid in Edward's classes at Amherst College. This remarkable body of work established Orra as one of America's first female scientific illustrators.

The house where Edward grew up is an attractive if modest structure. As originally built, it was one and a half stories with a gambrel roof and a small lean-to projecting from the rear. At some point in the early nineteenth century, it was

Orra White Hitchcock illustration from *Herbarium Parvum Pictum*

The Little Brown House

enlarged to the present two stories. When Deerfield Academy purchased the house in 1920, it commissioned the firm of Kirkham & Parlett to design a large dining room addition to the rear—this was one of Boyden's early projects before he embarked on more ambitious undertakings, such as the Main School Building. The dining hall behind Hitchcock House remained in use until the current Dining Hall was constructed in 1948. At that time, the ell was replaced by a smaller lean-to, creating the current saltbox form, and the house was used as a dormitory and faculty residence. It remained that way until 2001, when it was renovated once again to serve as the Academy bookstore.

33 The Little Brown House

Builder unknown, ca. 1783; restored by Deerfield Academy, 1953, 2012

Directly to the west of Hitchcock House sits a diminutive cottage known as the Little Brown House. Built for David Sexton in 1786, the house was owned by members of the Hitchcock family for much of the nineteenth century. In 1890, it was sold to Annie Putnam of Boston, who would later also purchase and restore the Manse with Madeline Wynne. Putnam renovated the Little Brown House for use as an art studio, installing an enormous dormer in the roof to admit natural light for painting.

In 1915, the Fullers, a family known for artistic talent, purchased the house. The most famous of the Fullers was the painter George Fuller. A Deerfield native, George had attended Deerfield Academy in 1839 before becoming a professional artist. A number of his paintings now reside in the collections of the Museum of Fine

Arts in Boston and the Metropolitan Museum in New York. George's son Arthur, also a painter, used the Little Brown House as a studio until 1945.

Deerfield Academy purchased the house in 1953 and restored it to its original eighteenth-century appearance by removing the dormer. The Little Brown House has served ever since as a faculty residence.

34 Allen House

Builder unknown, 1734; restored by Helen and Henry Flynt, 1945

The Allen House was built in 1734 for Thomas Bardwell, but it is named for the family that lived there from the mid-nineteenth century until the 1940s. Two notable family members were sisters Mary and Frances Allen, both of whom attended Deerfield Academy in the 1860s and lived in the Allen House from 1895 to 1941.

The sisters made a distinguished career together as photographers. (See pages 18–19.) Their work is wide-ranging and includes local images of the village, its residents, and the surrounding landscape, as well as photographs taken while travelling across the United States and in Europe. One of their distinctive genres is the re-creation of scenes from life in colonial New England. These photographs, which sometimes used their own house as a backdrop, formed part of the broader revival of interest in local history and traditional crafts—led by fellow residents Madeline Wynne and Annie Putnam, among others—that flourished in Deerfield around the turn of the twentieth century.

Both Allen sisters died in 1941. In 1945, their house was purchased by a family that would have an even more profound impact on the restoration and preservation of Deerfield's colonial heritage. Henry and Helen Flynt first became interested in Deerfield in 1936, when they enrolled their son Henry Jr. at the Academy. Henry Sr., a native of the nearby town of Monson and a graduate of Williams College, had a keen appreciation for New England history and took an immediate interest in the many attractive but dilapidated old houses lining the Street. Soon, to the delight of Frank Boyden, the Flynts began purchasing and restoring these old houses to rent or donate to the Academy, which was then in need of additional housing for both students and faculty. Among their first acquisitions in the 1940s were the Deerfield Inn, the Ashley House, and the Allen House, which, in a sign of their growing personal investment in Deerfield, they purchased for themselves. They soon followed these purchases with many other philanthropic projects that simultaneously furthered the cause of historic preservation and the educational mission of the Academy. These included renovations to the Manse, Hitchcock House, the Little Brown House, and John Williams House.

Eventually the Flynts' preservation efforts expanded beyond their projects for the Academy, and they ended up purchasing and restoring many of the town's houses in order to open them to the public as museums of early American history. What began as something of a personal hobby for the Flynts eventually resulted in the establishment in 1952 of the Heritage Foundation, which in 1971 became Historic

Allen House

Deerfield. Today, this nationally renowned museum maintains a dozen such houses, each of which has been painstakingly researched, restored, and authentically furnished. Not only does Historic Deerfield contribute to an unmatched educational and aesthetic setting for Deerfield Academy, but every year it attracts tens of thousands of visitors who are eager to experience the town's history and architecture. The Flynts' grandson, William Flynt (class of 1971), later carried on their work and only recently retired after a four-decade career as Historic Deerfield's architectural conservator.

Although Historic Deerfield is known today for its rigorous standards of historical authenticity, Henry and Helen were not professionally trained historians or curators. Consequently, many of their early restoration projects are now considered rather freewheeling. They felt that the most significant era in Deerfield's history was the colonial period, and their goal was to strip away later changes and modifications in order to restore houses—and indeed the entire village—to an original mid-eighteenth-century appearance. Complete historical accuracy was not always possible when it came to the reconstruction of lost original features—in those cases, they filled the gaps with plausible versions of what might have been so as to complete the aesthetic unity of the experience.

The Allen House is a prime example of this approach. Though originally constructed in 1734, the house had been thoroughly renovated in the 1830s. The original center chimney had been removed to make way for a central hall and staircase, and new chimneys had been built, one on either side, to serve the reconfigured rooms. On the exterior, the original door surround had been replaced by a later design. The Flynts, who considered nineteenth-century architecture to be of lesser value, removed all of this and attempted to reconstruct the house in its earlier configuration.

They were aided in this endeavor by William Gass, a local restoration contractor and Deerfield Academy alumnus, who would eventually oversee a majority of the Flynts' restoration projects. Gass relied on scraps of physical evidence remaining in the old houses and on his extensive knowledge of other colonial houses in the region. Paint marks on the old boards, for example, might reveal the original profiles of moldings or the former locations of interior partitions. But in many cases, the evidence was incomplete, leaving Gass to invent details using the techniques and stylistic sensibility of colonial builders. The design of the original front door surround of the Allen House, for example, was impossible to know, so the Flynts had Gass design and build a new one based on other houses from the same period. Thanks to Gass's skill, the result is highly convincing; like much of the interior, however, it is almost entirely conjectural and should properly be considered historically appropriate rather than historically accurate.

The other factor affecting the accuracy of the Allen House restoration was that it was not restored as a museum per se but as the Flynts' own part-time residence. Only in the 1970s did Historic Deerfield open it to the public. The museum decided to preserve the house as the Flynts had arranged it: a thoughtful but highly personal restoration, furnished with their eclectic collections and incorporating some modern conveniences. The result is a charmingly evocative portrait of the Flynts and their enthusiasm for bringing back to life the spirit and ambiance of colonial New England.

Historic Deerfield offers guided tours of this house.

35 Sheldon House

Builders unknown, 1754–57; addition, 1802; restored by Helen and Henry Flynt, 1948

The Sheldon House was built between 1754 and 1757 for John Sheldon III. He was the grandson of Ensign John Sheldon, who survived the French and Indian raid of 1704 (discussed in Walk Five, page 174). The Sheldon family lived in the house for almost two centuries, until 1946, when Henry and Helen Flynt purchased it first for use by Deerfield Academy and then as one of Historic Deerfield's museum houses.

The most notable resident of the house was George Sheldon, the town's venerable historian. Sheldon looked the part: photographs from the early twentieth century show a tall, bald man with spectacles nestled on a beaked nose between bushy eyebrows, the image completed by a tapering, waist-length silver beard. He had attended the Academy in 1839 and developed a deep appreciation of local history. Less than a decade later, he participated in Reverend Willard's unsuccessful efforts to save the Old Indian House (built by George's great-great-great-grandfather in 1699). His primary occupation during his early years was farming; a severe case of sunstroke in 1853 limited his capacity for field labor, however, giving him more time to pursue his study of history. He founded the Pocumtuck Valley Memorial Association (PVMA) in 1870 and served as its president until his death in 1916, organizing its annual meetings and contributing numerous articles on local history to its printed *Proceedings*. When Deerfield Academy moved to the newly constructed Dickinson High School building in 1878, Sheldon was instrumental in saving the original Academy Building, which he transformed into the Memorial Hall Museum. This museum was furnished with a large collection of local artifacts, many of which Sheldon had assembled over the preceding years—it was rumored that he routinely entered the houses of neighbors while they were out in order to rummage through their attics and "rescue" any neglected historic artifacts he might find. (See Walk One, page 27.) Sheldon's most substantial written work, *A History of Deerfield, Massachusetts*, was published in two volumes in 1895–1896 and remains the most exhaustive account of the town's early years.

George Sheldon's second wife, Jennie Maria Arms Sheldon, was also active in the PVMA. In 1913, she took over as curator of the museum, and in 1929 she became the association's president, holding both posts until her death in 1938. Although she shared George's interest in history, as noted in Walks One and Two, Jennie's primary intellectual pursuit was science; over time, she made numerous gifts to Deerfield Academy, including a building to support girls' education (the Girls Club) and a new science building (the Arms Building).

Architecturally, the Sheldon House is a quintessential mid-eighteenth-century design. Its handsome front door and surround are original and a fine example of the style popular in the Connecticut River Valley at the time. It shares many features with John Williams House, though it is somewhat less elaborate. The first-floor windows are capped by pediments, echoing that of the door surround, and the nine-pane window sashes installed in the 1948 restoration are an accurate reconstruction of the originals. The slight projection of the wall in the gable ends, just above the second-floor windows, is a late vestige of seventeenth-century building practices. The one-and-a-half-story ell with gambrel roof was added in 1802. This is one of several similar gambrel-roofed ells in Deerfield constructed around the turn of the nineteenth century. They are thought to reflect a Connecticut building tradition brought to Deerfield in 1797 by housewright William Russell of Wethersfield.

Historic Deerfield offers guided tours of this house.

36 Ashley House

Builder unknown, 1734; restored by Helen and Henry Flynt, 1948

Earlier in this walk, we witnessed the revolutionary patriotism of Colonel Joseph Stebbins. The Ashley House, at the far northern end of the Street, offers a glimpse of the opposing political viewpoint of Reverend Jonathan Ashley, town minister and an ardent Tory.

Sheldon House

Having led Deerfield's Congregational Church since 1732, Ashley was one of the town's most prominent and respected citizens. In the lead-up to the revolution, however, as Whigs gained political traction, Ashley's steadfast loyalty to the crown increasingly put him at odds with the rest of the community. In 1774, the town voted to eliminate his salary and firewood allowance, and at least one attempt was made to officially unseat him as the town minister. The indefatigable Ashley continued in his post (largely unpaid, apparently) until his death in 1780, and it seems that he never shied away from giving voice to his political convictions. George Sheldon, in his 1896 *A History of Deerfield, Massachusetts*, relates the following: "When Parson Ashley finished reading from the pulpit the first proclamation ending with the customary 'God save the Commonwealth of Massachusetts,' he rose to his full height and with stentorian tones added 'And the King, too, I say, or we are an undone people.'"

Ashley's house was built in 1734, shortly after he arrived in Deerfield to assume leadership of the church. In its original configuration, it had a simple pitched roof with a central chimney; the current gambrel roof and center hall configuration date from a renovation done in 1780, not long after Ashley's death.

In 1869, Ashley's descendants had a new house built on the site and moved the original house to the back of the property, relegating it to use as a barn. (See Walk Three, page 114.) By the early twentieth century, the old house had lost its original windows, doors, chimneys, and most of its interior paneling and other

Ashley House

details. Nonetheless, in 1949, Henry and Helen Flynt purchased the dilapidated structure and enlisted contractor William Gass to restore the house to its eighteenth-century condition. As part of this project, they moved the house back to its original site. To make way for it, the 1869 Ashley House was moved down the street to Deerfield Academy's campus, where it served as a dormitory until its demolition in 2012.

As with their restoration of the Allen House, the Flynts and Gass had to reconstruct many missing elements of the old Ashley House based on evidence that was often fragmentary at best. For example, Gass designed the robust and elaborate front door surround by drawing inspiration from other mid-eighteenth-century doors in Deerfield and nearby towns; therefore, while stylistically appropriate and beautifully executed, it should be understood as purely conjectural.

Similarly, only one original interior wall remained, and the rest had to be completely reconstructed. Given the limited amount of original material, the overall effect of the reconstruction is remarkably convincing. Today, the house is fully furnished with New England antiques dating back to Ashley's lifetime and is open to the public.

Historic Deerfield offers guided tours of this house.

Ashley House, interior

Ashley House, interior

WALK FIVE

Deerfield and the Broader Community

37 Town Common

38 Old Burying Ground and 1704 Memorial

39 Old Indian House Memorial

40 Meetinghouses and Churches

a. Third Meetinghouse *(demolished)*

b. Fourth Meetinghouse *(demolished)*

c. The Brick Church

d. Deerfield Post Office

e. The White Church

41 Frary House and Barnard Tavern

42 Hall Tavern

43 Deerfield Inn

44 Eaglebrook School

45 Bement School

46 Nearby Towns and Cities

a. Greenfield, Massachusetts

b. Northampton, Massachusett

c. Amherst, Massachusetts

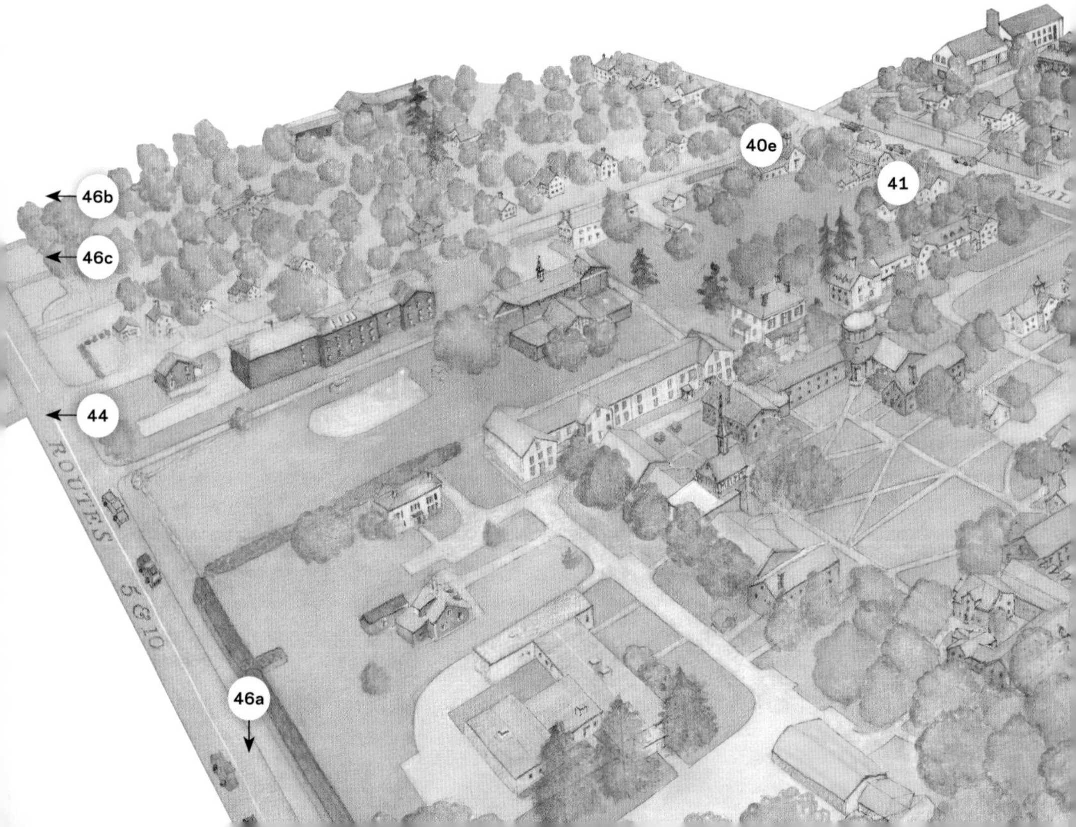

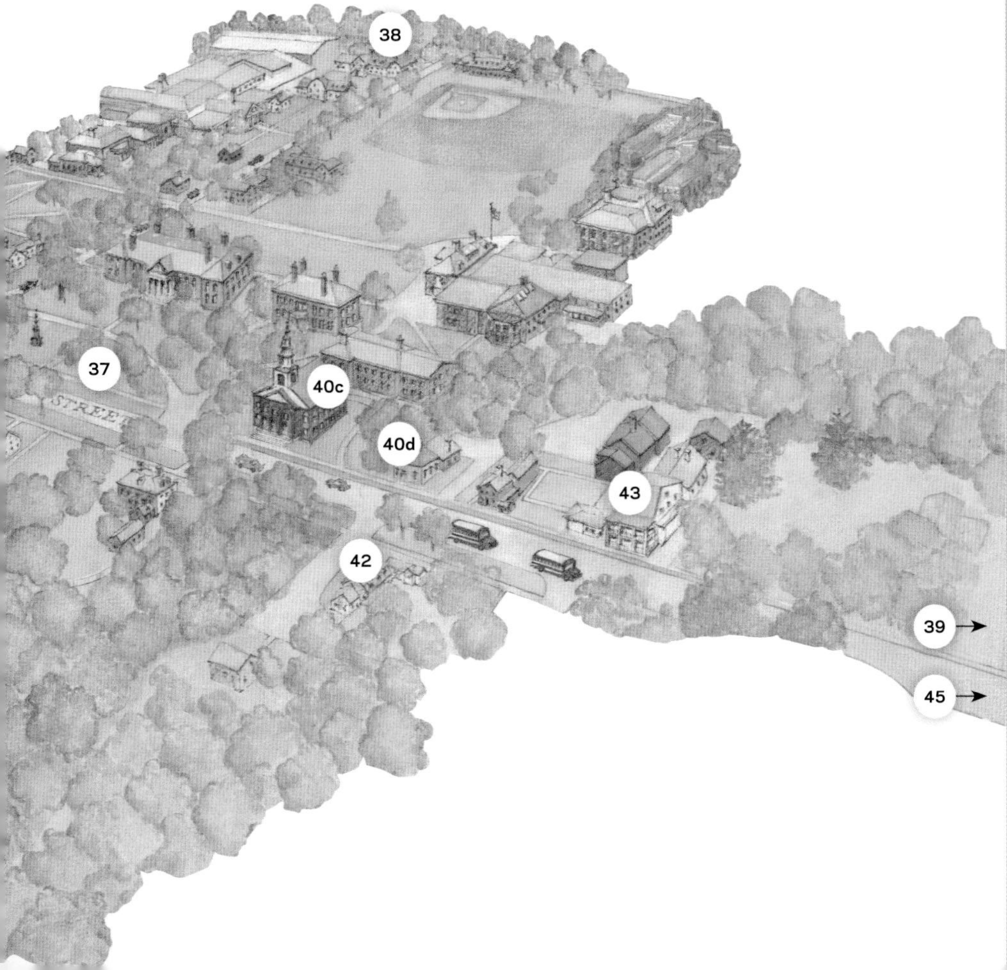
38
37
40c
40d
43
42
39 →
45 →

WALK FIVE

Deerfield and the Broader Community

Building on the preceding walk, Walk Five continues to expand beyond the Deerfield Academy campus into the broader community, exploring the village's defining civic buildings, monuments, and institutions and the ways in which they interact with the Academy.

Beginning at the center of the village, we examine the monuments and memorials of the Town Common and the Old Burying Ground, which recall pivotal chapters in the town's history. We then consider the town's religious life as manifested in its meetinghouses and churches. Next, we delve into the history of tourism and hospitality, stopping at two early taverns (now museums run by Historic Deerfield) and a nineteenth-century hotel that is still in operation in the village center. We also visit two independent junior boarding schools, Eaglebrook and Bement. All these institutions contribute in essential and complementary ways to the life of the community, and their buildings are salient features of the townscape. They also maintain strong relationships with Deerfield Academy and shape the experiences of the school's students, faculty, staff, and alumni.

The walk concludes with a brief description of the major towns and cities in the surrounding region—Greenfield, Northampton, and Amherst—weekend destinations for students and communities that embody the distinctive culture of the Connecticut River Valley.

37 Town Common

a. Old Fort Well, builder unknown, ca. 1690; capped ca. 1880
b. Civil War Memorial, Batterson Monumental Works, 1867

Like many New England towns, Deerfield was laid out with a common at its center—an open space shared by the entire community and used originally for grazing livestock and exercises by the local militia. This tree-shaded lawn now forms the heart of both the village and the Academy and is surrounded by some of the community's most important buildings: the Brick Church to the north, the Main School Building and Arms Building to the west, and across the street to the east, the Manse and three Academy dormitories.

At the outbreak of King William's War in 1690, the town constructed a stockade wall to defend against any attack by the French and their Native American allies. The wall was a ten-foot-high, tightly packed row of vertical timber posts. It enclosed a rectangular area that included the meetinghouse, the Town Common, and about a dozen dwellings. Despite the effort taken to build it and relocate many families to houses within its protective precinct, the wall ultimately proved ineffective during the French and Indian raid of 1704. The last vestiges of these fortifications were removed by the 1740s, and today all that remains from this period is the Old Fort Well, with its protruding stone cap added around 1880.

The Common's most prominent feature is the Civil War Memorial, one of the first of its kind in Massachusetts, erected in September 1867. It stands on a small earthen mound flanked by four carved sandstone piers that originally held a low iron fence. The monument itself is built of sandstone and consists of a pedestal surmounted by a square, tapering Doric pier. The pedestal bears a dedicatory inscription and the names of Deerfield men who died in the war, and the names of battlefields and prisons where they died are carved into horizontal bands on the pier's shaft. A life-size statue of a Union solider originally topped the monument, but natural deterioration of the stone over the course of 150 years led to its removal in 2015. It has now been conserved and is on display in the town office building in South Deerfield. A bronze replica of the statue was installed in the late spring of 2019 through donations and the joint efforts of the (town of) Deerfield Historical Commission and the Academy, including the Deerfield class of 1969 on the occasion of their fiftieth reunion.

38 Old Burying Ground and 1704 Memorial

Established before 1695; memorial mason unknown, 1901

One of Deerfield's less conspicuous historic sites is its Old Burying Ground. Established in the village's first years, it lies at the far western end of Albany Road on the edge of the plateau overlooking the Lower Level. The oldest headstone is that of Joseph Barnard (1641–1695), though earlier unmarked graves likely exist on the site. According to at least one reputable nineteenth-century source, a Native American burying yard lies on or near the same site. Most of the stones in the Old Burying Ground predate 1803, when a new cemetery (now known as the Laurel Hill Cemetery) was opened on the hillside east of town.

Most of the markers in the Old Burying Ground are carved of slate or sandstone, with rounded tops and shoulders. The most common decorative motifs are the death's head (a winged skull) and the cherub. Inscriptions tend to be simple, typified by this one on the headstone of the town's most famous minister:

> Here lyes ye Body of the Rev'd Mr. John Williams, the Beloved & Faithfull Pastor of this place, Who died on June ye 12, 1729, In the 65th Year of his Age. Rev. 13:14 Write, Blessed are ye Dead which die in the Lord.

The most prominent monument in the Old Burying Ground sits atop a large earthen mound traditionally believed to mark the grave of those who were killed in the French and Indian Raid of 1704. The monument, a simple cubic block with a shallow pyramidal top, was installed by C. (Charlotte) Alice Baker in 1901 and reads: "The grave of 48 men women and children, victims of the French and Indian raid on Deerfield, February 29, 1704."

Town Common, with Civil War Memorial

Old Burying Ground

This landmark recalls one of the most traumatic events in Deerfield's early history. At the outbreak of the French and Indian Wars in 1690, Deerfield was one of the farthest northwestern outposts of the English colonies in North America; as such, it became a prime target for the French and their Native American allies. In 1704, Massachusetts governor Joseph Dudley sent a garrison of twenty English soldiers to protect Deerfield, a measure that would prove futile. On the night of February 29, a raiding party of several hundred French, Mohawk, and Abenaki soldiers, having trekked more than three hundred miles from Canada, took the English soldiers and the town's inhabitants by surprise.

Heavy snows had drifted up against the stockade wall that winter, allowing the attackers to climb over the fortifications and past the guard, who was asleep at his post. The invaders set fire to many of the houses inside the fort and attacked the panicked townspeople. By the time English reinforcements arrived from the neighboring towns of Hatfield and Hadley, nearly fifty of Deerfield's 291 inhabitants had been killed and another 109 had been taken prisoner.

The attackers took their captives, including Deerfield's minister, Reverend John Williams, to Canada. For several years, Governor Dudley of Massachusetts and Governor Vaudreuil of New France negotiated the exchange of prisoners. Eventually, fifty-nine of the eighty-three Deerfield captives who had survived the march north returned to Massachusetts. The rest, mostly children, remained in Canada, where they were assimilated into French or Native American communities. Reverend Williams was among those who returned to Deerfield, where he served as minister

John Williams headstone

1704 Memorial

once again from 1707 until his death in 1729. He described both the raid and his subsequent experiences in Canada in a highly popular book, *The Redeemed Captive Returning to Zion* (1707).

We know as much as we do about the 1704 raid in no small part thanks to C. Alice Baker, the woman who installed the grave marker. Baker grew up in western Massachusetts and attended Deerfield Academy from 1849 to 1850—one of only two girls at the time. After graduating, she taught at a school in Illinois and then at Deerfield Academy. In 1856, along with her lifelong companion, Susan Minot Lane, Baker opened a school for girls in Chicago. Eight years later, the two returned to Cambridge to care for Baker's ailing mother, opening another girls' school in Boston. They spent their summers in Deerfield, where Baker developed her interest in the 1704 raid. She researched the event extensively, traveling to Canada several times to pore through official records and visit Native American missions. She was eventually able to identify many of the Deerfield captives and even discover some of their fates.

Regarded as an expert in New England history, she delivered several papers to the Pocumtuck Valley Memorial Association (PVMA), of which she was an active member, and authored a book, *True Stories of New England Captives Carried to Canada during the Old French and Indian Wars* (1897). Baker is also remembered for her historic preservation work, in particular her efforts to restore her own home, the Frary House.

39 Old Indian House Memorial

William Gass, 1929

Although much of the town burned during the attack of 1704, several houses survived. Among them was the large, centrally positioned house of Ensign John Sheldon. Sheldon and his family managed to fend off the French and Native American attackers for the duration of the raid, although his wife, Hannah, was shot and killed after the attackers managed to chop a hole in the heavy front door just large enough to fire a musket through. The house, which came to be known as the Old Indian House, survived well into the nineteenth century, long enough to be documented by an early photograph in the 1840s. Unfortunately, despite a valiant campaign to save it led by Reverend Willard, the house was demolished in 1848. Town residents salvaged the hatchet-scarred front door and several ornamental trim pieces as historic relics. These have been preserved and can be viewed today in the Memorial Hall Museum.

In addition to its dramatic role in the 1704 raid, the house was notable from an architectural standpoint. Built in 1699, it was a prime example of the postmedieval building style of the early colonies. This style predates the influence of Georgian classicism and takes most of its design cues instead from the buildings of medieval England. The most distinctive feature of houses from this period is the overhang of the second story beyond the footprint of the first story, and of the attic, in turn, over the second story. American houses of this period generally display little in the way of ornament; however, the Old Indian House did feature carved wood brackets

to visually support the overhanging second floor, and the central chimney included some ornamental brickwork. As was typical, the Old Indian House had few windows and those it did have were small: glass was costly and a risk to security.

In 1929, William Gass built a replica of the Old Indian House, now owned by the PVMA. The reconstruction is not on the original site—which is currently occupied by the Kendall Classroom Building—but farther north along the Street. The exterior is an accurate reproduction of the original building. The house is open to visitors.

40 Meetinghouses and Churches

a. Third Meetinghouse, builder unknown, 1695; demolished, after 1730
b. Fourth Meetinghouse, Jonas Locke, 1729; remodeled, builder unknown, 1766; demolished, 1824
c. The Brick Church, Winthrop Clapp, 1824
d. Deerfield Post Office, architect unknown, 1912; remodeled by Helen and Henry Flynt (based on the Third Meetinghouse, 1695), 1952
e. The White Church (Orthodox Congregational Church), architect unknown, 1838; restored with addition by Historic Deerfield, 1957

Deerfield Academy is a secular institution, and unlike many of its peer boarding schools, it has never had its own dedicated chapel. The school does have a spiritual focal point, though, which it shares with the village: the First Church of Deerfield, also known as the Brick Church. For many years, student attendance at weekly services was mandatory, and although this is no longer the case for the Academy's diverse student body, the church continues to welcome students. The church also hosts an annual baccalaureate service for the senior class just before graduation.

Built in 1824, the Brick Church is Deerfield's fifth meetinghouse. The first four were constructed in 1675, 1682, 1695, and 1729, respectively, and stood in the center of the Common, on or near the place where the Civil War monument is today. Little is known of the design of the first two meetinghouses, though they were likely small and simple structures designed for utility rather than beauty. The third meetinghouse, built in 1695, was constructed to be the same size as one in nearby Hatfield, about thirty feet square. A visitor to Deerfield in 1728 documented the design in a very rough sketch that shows a two-story building capped by a hipped roof with a central, multitiered cupola. Town records from the period indicate that a three-sided balcony, or gallery, with three rows of seats on each side was completed by 1701.

This general configuration would align it with many other seventeenth-century New England meetinghouses. In conventional churches, the seating is oriented toward an altar at one end of a long axis, but the radical Puritans preferred an arrangement in which the seating focused inward toward a central pulpit, creating an atmosphere more like an auditorium than a church. Such a configuration emphasized the communal aspect of Puritan worship and allowed the building to be used for secular town meetings as well as Sunday services. It also had the advantage of

OPPOSITE **Old Indian House Memorial**

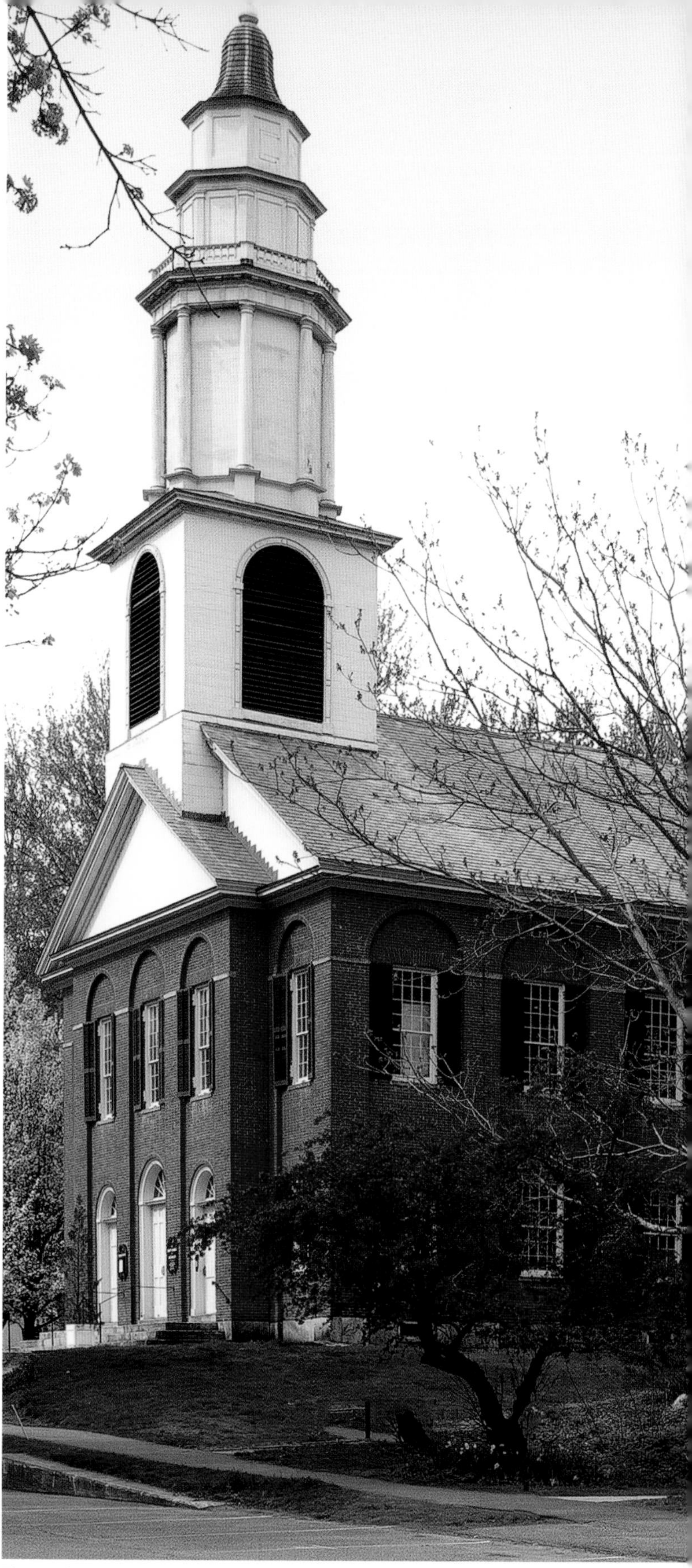

The Brick Church and post office

UNITED STATES POST OFFICE
75

The Brick Church, entrance detail

bringing congregants as close as possible to the minister so they would not miss a word of his sermons.

The third meetinghouse was demolished sometime after 1730, but we can get an approximate sense for the building by looking at the Deerfield post office, just north of the Brick Church. Though this building was built in 1912, Henry and Helen Flynt renovated it in 1952 so that it would resemble the 1695 meetinghouse structure (though with only one story rather than two). Thus, the post office now incorporates a number of characteristics of local seventeenth-century architecture, such as the small leaded-glass casement windows. It is capped by a plausible, if conjectural, reconstruction of the meetinghouse cupola.

In 1729, the town built the fourth meetinghouse. At forty by fifty feet, it was significantly larger than the third meetinghouse, but it still featured a central cupola, three-sided gallery, and the pulpit centered on the long west side. (An extensive description of this meetinghouse, including the design of the interior, is given by George Sheldon in *A History of Deerfield, Massachusetts*, pages 471–81.) The building was substantially remodeled in 1766–1767, at which time the cupola was replaced with a new steeple added on to the northern gable end. A nineteenth-century drawing by Nathaniel Hitchcock indicates that the main east entrance (possibly dating from the 1767 renovation) featured an elaborate surround with a scrolled pediment, similar to the one found on the 1760 John Williams House.

The Brick Church, interior

This building remained until 1824, when, under the leadership of the Reverend Samuel Willard, the town replaced it with the fifth and current meetinghouse, the Brick Church. (See Walk Four, page 149.) The architect, Winthrop Clapp, closely modeled the new meetinghouse on one that had recently been designed by Isaac Damon in nearby Greenfield.

It is a graceful neoclassical structure, built of brick with a wood steeple. The exterior walls are enlivened by a series of shallow two-story recessed arches within which are set large double-hung windows with louvered shutters. The main facade is five bays wide, with the center three grouped together in a slightly projecting frontispiece capped by a wood pediment that nests pleasingly within the larger gable. The steeple rises from the pediment in four tiers: the first is square with large louvered arches, and the second is octagonal with a fully articulated Doric colonnade and a low balustrade. The third and fourth tiers, also octagonal, become progressively smaller and simpler, terminating in a bell-shaped roof. The gilded weathercock at the top was first built for the 1729 meetinghouse and reused here.

The interior configuration of the church marks a significant departure from Deerfield's early meetinghouses. Instead of the old centralized plan, the Brick Church follows a more conventional arrangement in which the whole congregation faces in the same direction, toward the pulpit at the east end. Because the church is positioned on the west side of the Street, the front entrance must be placed at

The White Church

the church's east end, the same end as the pulpit. The somewhat odd result is that from the entrance vestibule, one passes into the sanctuary through one of two doors flanking the pulpit and facing the rest of the congregation.

The sanctuary itself is a spare, whitewashed box with a slightly domed ceiling. The original box pews remain and face a classical mahogany pulpit (added later) set within a shallow niche. A balcony supported by Tuscan columns runs around three sides of the space. It contains a pipe organ built in 2003 by Richards, Fowkes & Co. The beautifully crafted organ case of carved and gilded woodwork is a surprising moment of Baroque opulence in this otherwise prim New England meetinghouse.

As dramatic a change as the Brick Church was from the older meetinghouse, its impact was overshadowed by the theological revolution instituted by Reverend Willard, who converted the congregation to Unitarianism when he arrived in 1807. In response, a conservative faction broke away to form a new Orthodox Congregational Church, which raised its own building on Memorial Street in 1838. Constructed of wood and known as the White Church (to distinguish it from the Brick Church), the

Frary House and Barnard Tavern

building is a modest example of the Greek Revival style. Its most distinctive feature is a charming square steeple crowned by four tapered finials.

Deerfield's two congregations reunited in 1931, and today the Brick Church shares an affiliation with both the United Church of Christ (Congregational) and the Unitarian Universalist Association. Historic Deerfield acquired and restored the White Church in 1957 and continues to maintain it as an events venue.

41 Frary House and Barnard Tavern

Builder unknown, ca. 1760, with tavern addition, 1795; restored by C. Alice Baker, 1890; restored by Helen and Henry Flynt, ca. 1950

The Frary House and attached Barnard Tavern sit on the east side of the Street, just south of Pocumtuck Dormitory. There is some uncertainty as to the original date of construction—houses are documented on the lot from as early as the 1690s—but it is now thought that Nathaniel Frary built the earliest surviving portion of the house, the northern five bays facing the street, around 1760. Salah Barnard had the large southern tavern wing added shortly before his death in 1795. The resulting long facade is characteristic of New England inns and public houses in the eighteenth century, another typical example being the Hall Tavern.

The second floor of the tavern addition features a large ballroom with a vaulted plaster ceiling and built-in benches running along both sides. The elegant fireplace at the east end of this room is flanked by a pair of arched recesses and is a fine example of Federal design. At the opposite end of the ballroom, a small, elevated alcove is designed to accommodate musicians for dances.

In 1797, only a few years after the room's construction, it hosted the first meeting of Deerfield Academy's trustees. This group continued to meet at the

Barnard Tavern, ballroom

Barnard Tavern over the subsequent months to plan for the new school, including the acquisition of property—one acre of land for $333—and the design and construction of the Academy Building.

By the late nineteenth century, after a period of neglect, the Frary House was severely deteriorated. As with the Manse five years earlier, it was two Boston women who stepped in to save it: C. Alice Baker and Susan Minot Lane. Baker, a historian of the 1704 French and Indian raid on Deerfield, was a descendant of the Frary family. Persuaded by her cousin, Deerfield historian George Sheldon, Baker purchased and renovated the dilapidated house in 1890. Sheldon also advised her on the restoration, although Baker likely needed little encouragement, as she had already demonstrated her passion for historic preservation by partaking in the successful campaign to save Boston's Old South Meetinghouse in 1879.

Baker hired the Boston architectural firm of Shepley, Rutan & Coolidge to oversee the renovation work, but she remained closely involved in the project. For example, she personally selected each of the antique bricks, handing them, one by one, to the mason as he rebuilt the chimney. Her restoration was in the spirit of the early Colonial Revival—aimed not at historical precision but at creating an artistic impression of colonial antiquity. Accordingly, she incorporated various architectural fragments that she had collected from other houses and introduced antique furnishings from a variety of historical periods.

Once the project was complete, Baker and her partner, Susan Minot Lane, spent summers at the house, and as noted earlier, Baker became an active participant in the PVMA and chronicler of the town's history. On her death in 1909, she willed the Frary House to the PVMA to preserve as a museum. In the late 1940s, the house was restored again for the PVMA by Henry and Helen Flynt, who sought (with only limited success) to re-create more authentically colonial interiors. In the 1960s, the Heritage Foundation (the precursor to Historic Deerfield) acquired the house, and it has been operated as one of its museum houses ever since. Today, the Barnard Tavern section is once again undergoing a restoration, the latest attempt to correct earlier restorations and bring the house closer to its original condition.

Historic Deerfield offers guided tours of this house.

42 Hall Tavern

Builders unknown, 1760, with addition, ca. 1800; moved from Charlemont to Deerfield and restored by Henry and Helen Flynt, 1949

The early history of the Hall Tavern is analogous to that of the Barnard Tavern: it comprises a saltbox house of about 1785, which was extended on one side around 1815 to create spaces for public gatherings. Despite the similarities, the Hall and Barnard Taverns were never direct competitors because the Hall Tavern was built about twenty miles to the west, in the town of Charlemont. Henry and Helen Flynt moved the building to Deerfield in 1949 and renovated it to serve as a museum and visitors center, a role it still serves today. The Hall Tavern is one of only a handful of houses along the Street that are not original to Deerfield. The other two are Dwight House, built in Springfield, and a saltbox house from Conway.

Centrally located and across the street from the Deerfield Inn, the Hall Tavern is the first stop for anyone interested in visiting Historic Deerfield's various properties along the Street. Here, one can find introductory information about the village and its museums, view an orientation video, and purchase tickets for events and house tours. The tavern also houses several restored and furnished rooms, including a ballroom similar to that of the Barnard Tavern, and a kitchen, used now for demonstrations of eighteenth-century open-hearth cooking.

As with other early restorations by the Flynts, such as the Allen and Ashley Houses, much of the Hall Tavern had to be reconstructed from scratch, often with little solid evidence as a guide. On the exterior, the door surrounds and window pediments are the work of contractor William Gass, who executed most of the Flynts' restoration projects.

43 Deerfield Inn

Architect unknown, 1884; renovated by Henry and Helen Flynt, 1945

The Deerfield Inn is the only hotel still operating in the village's historic center. It was built in 1884 by George Arms, father of Jennie Arms Sheldon, who ran the inn with her sister for several years after George's death in 1897. (See Walk One, page 43; Walk Two, page 72; and Walk Four, page 161.) The establishment changed hands

Hall Tavern

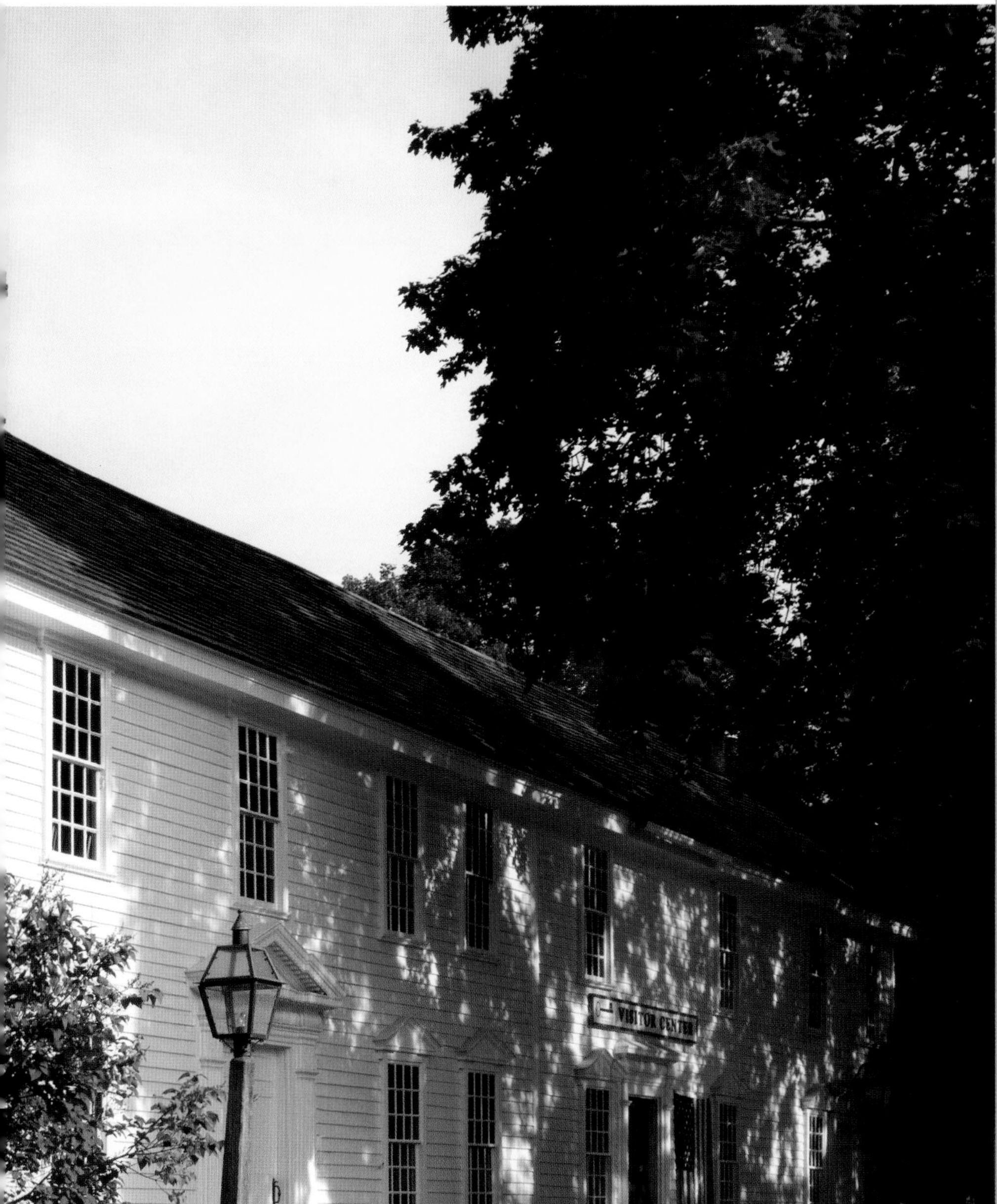
VISITOR CENTER

DEERFIELD
INN

a number of times in the early twentieth century, until eventually Henry and Helen Flynt purchased and renovated it in 1945.

Originally called the Pocumtuck Hotel (from 1884 until 1914), the inn was the successor to a series of hotels that had stood on the site where Pocumtuck Dormitory is now. The first establishment at that location was a tavern that served the town from 1805 until 1853, when it was replaced by the three-story hotel known first as the Pocumtuck House and later as the Pocumtuck Hotel. This building burned in 1877, but in 1881 an even larger hotel, the Everett House, was constructed on the same site. A four-story Italianate building, it had fifty guest rooms, a one-hundred-seat dining room, and a ballroom. Unfortunately, the impressive hotel burned down in 1883, only two years after its construction. Its owners did not rebuild after the fire, leaving an opening for George Arms to open his own hotel down the street in 1884.

Although the new Pocumtuck Hotel was significantly smaller than the Everett House, it shared a similar architectural style. The dominant feature of both was a double-decker wraparound porch, which offered summer guests a shaded and breezy place to relax, socialize, and observe the daily life of the Street. The most ornamental feature on the hotel building, the porches comprised two tiers of finely detailed square columns set on pedestals linked by delicate wood railings, a style very similar to the porches on Bewkes House.

This Italianate detailing, however, did not fit the Flynts' Colonial Revival aesthetic, and in their 1945 renovation they rebuilt the porch using four double-height round columns and simplified railings. To complete the Colonial Revival transformation, they also replaced the original two-over-two windows with smaller-paned sashes and installed a new Federal-style door with sidelights and a fanlight. They remodeled the interior along similar stylistic lines.

Today, Historic Deerfield owns the inn, which remains popular with visitors to both the museum and Deerfield Academy. In addition to twenty-four guest rooms, it features an elegant restaurant and tavern known as Champney's.

44 Eaglebrook School

Founded 1922, various architects

In 1922, Howard Gibbs, an Amherst College graduate, former faculty member at Deerfield Academy, and friend of Headmaster Frank Boyden, founded a second boarding school in town. The Eaglebrook School enrolls younger boys, grades six through nine. Gibbs was succeeded as headmaster by three generations of the Chase family, who have overseen the growth of the school into a community of 250 students coming from across the country and around the world. Historically, many graduates of Eaglebrook have gone on to attend Deerfield Academy, joining the school as sophomores.

Eaglebrook's 800-acre campus sits on the flank of Pocumtuck Ridge, east of the town center. The oldest building on campus is the Lodge. Built in the late nineteenth century, the former sanatorium and hunting camp now serves as the

OPPOSITE: **Deerfield Inn**

Eaglebrook School

administrative center. Most of Eaglebrook's buildings, however, were constructed during the second half of the twentieth century: five dormitories, a dining hall, four classroom buildings, faculty houses, an athletics center, a hockey rink, and a pool. The school also maintains its own alpine ski area a little ways up the hill.

Eaglebrook has commissioned Windigo Architects of Morristown, New Jersey, to design many recent projects. Among these are two new dormitories and the extensive renovation of three older dorms, as well as the new hockey rink, squash courts, pool, and the Evans Center for science, art, and music. For these projects, Windigo has established an architectural character that blends modernist forms with traditional materials, paying particular attention to the way in which the buildings are visually integrated with the landscape. Windigo has also completed a renovation of the original Lodge and of the Chase Learning Center, which was designed in 1965 by the Architects' Collaborative.

The Eaglebrook campus has an informal plan, its buildings oriented in harmony with the natural contours of the land. Many buildings are loosely grouped around the central Gates Lawn and Whipple Pond, while others are nestled discreetly into the wooded hillside.

45 Bement School

Founded 1925, various architects

In 1925, three years after the founding of Eaglebrook School, Grace Bement opened Deerfield's third private school, this one for boys and girls in kindergarten through ninth grade. Bement had moved to Deerfield from Framingham, Massachusetts, in 1920, when her husband, Lewis Bement, took up a position as head of the John Russell Cutlery Company in nearby Turners Falls, Massachusetts. Grace taught English and drama for several years at Deerfield Academy, and in 1923, she began tutoring younger students in the living room of the couple's house on the Street. This structure, now known as Bement House and containing the school's dining hall, is one of the oldest in Deerfield. It was built by Joseph Severance around 1712 and substantially remodeled in 1825.

In its first full year of operation, the Bement School had a class of seven students, a number that quickly grew, prompting Grace to renovate a stable behind the house and add another building, the circa 1840 Snively House, for use by the school. Grace had Snively moved to the school property from the town of Enfield, one of

Bement School

four central Massachusetts towns that were being dismantled at the time to make way for the Quabbin Reservoir. In 1930, when the school began accepting boarding students, it acquired the 1825 Barton House next door for a dormitory. About this time, Grace also renovated the large barn on the property to serve as a multipurpose theater and auditorium, a function it still serves. She continued to run the school until her retirement in 1947, at which point she and Lewis moved into Snively House, now home to the school's Alumni and Development Office.

Today, the Bement School has both a lower and an upper school, with a combined total of about 180 day students and 45 boarders who come from around the world. From its the cosmopolitan student body, the school succeeds in creating a tightly knit community. The school seeks to integrate students from different grades as much as possible and brings all students together for daily assemblies in the Barn and for family-style meals in the Bement House dining room. The rigorous academic program is supplemented by a wide range of cocurricular activities and enriched by field trips to nearby museums, theaters, and festivals in Deerfield, Shelburne Falls, and Northampton, and the more distant towns of the Berkshires.

In recent decades, the campus has continued to expand along with the growing student body. The Polk Building, added in 1967, originally housed the upper school and library, and now, after extensive renovations by Kuhn Riddle Architects, serves as the school library. In the 1990s and 2000s, Margot Jones of Jones Whitsett Architects in Greenfield designed new lower and upper school buildings, both of which feature traditional timber-frame construction echoing the rustic aesthetic of the old Barn.

Between 2010 and 2012, Margot Jones also completed two new dormitories, located about a five-minute walk from the main campus at the northern end of the Street and near the Italianate Haas House of 1849 (also a Bement dormitory). The architecture of these recent projects has followed a simple New England vernacular style: rambling clapboarded structures that seek to harmonize with Deerfield's colonial houses and outbuildings. Like Deerfield Academy and Eaglebrook, Bement has endeavored in recent years to moderate the environmental impact of its new buildings, focusing on energy efficiency and the use of renewable energy sources.

46 Nearby Towns and Cities

a. Greenfield, Massachusetts, incorporated 1753
b. Northampton, Massachusetts, chartered 1653
c. Amherst, Massachusetts, incorporated 1759

Deerfield Academy's rural setting is admirable for its seclusion: the quiet village and bucolic valley form an ideal environment for the development of a strong and cohesive school community. While remote from much of the outside world, Deerfield is just a ten-minute drive to several thriving small cities along the Connecticut River, including Greenfield, Northampton, and Amherst. These larger centers of education, commerce, arts, and entertainment offer a lively counterpoint to the cloistered ambiance of the Pocumtuck Valley, and students often make the trip on weekends to visit their theaters, concert halls, and restaurants.

All three communities are notable for the economic and cultural vitality of their historic downtowns, a rarity in an age when local businesses face competition from national chains, malls, and internet retailers. Shops and restaurants are fueled in part by tourism, as well as by students who come to study at several prestigious colleges in the area. These forces also contribute to a dynamic culture of art, music, and theater, supported by numerous galleries, theaters, and museums. The three cities are each as rich in history and architectural character as Deerfield, and this guide is able to offer only brief overviews by way of introduction and to suggest avenues for further exploration.

Greenfield is Deerfield's closest neighbor to the north and was, in fact, originally part of Deerfield, splitting off to form a separate town in 1753. By the early nineteenth century, it had surpassed Deerfield in prominence, and in 1811 it became the county seat of newly formed Franklin County. During the following decades, Greenfield's position at the junction of the Deerfield and Connecticut rivers enabled it to develop into a center of commerce and industry, a boom that was further fueled by the arrival of the railroad in the 1840s. Like many American towns and cities, Greenfield experienced a decline in the mid-twentieth century; however, in recent years its downtown has started to revitalize, and several historic buildings have now been refurbished. The city's population today is just over 17,000.

Downtown Greenfield includes several fine examples of nineteenth-century civic and commercial architecture, especially around Court Square at

Bank Row and Main Street, Greenfield, Massachusetts

the intersection of Main Street and Bank Row. Of particular note is the stately and well-preserved 1813 Franklin County Courthouse at 15 Bank Row (currently occupied by the Connecticut River Conservancy). Of a completely different architectural character, the robust art deco building next door was constructed in 1929 for the First National Bank & Trust Company. At the corner of Main and Federal Streets sits an impressive example of Beaux-Arts architecture: the former Franklin Savings Bank, built in 1911 and now home to the Pushkin Gallery.

Greenfield boasts two notable Federal-period houses by architect Asher Benjamin, completed shortly before he designed Deerfield's original Academy Building: the splendid Coleman-Hollister House of 1796 sits on a rise overlooking Bank Row, and the Greenfield Public Library occupies the 1797 Leavitt-Hovey House at 402 Main Street. Some of Greenfield's finest nineteenth-century residential architecture can be found at the east end of Main Street and further along High Street, including excellent examples of Greek Revival, Italianate, Queen Anne, and other Victorian styles.

About fifteen miles to the south of Deerfield is Northampton, settled in 1654 and the oldest city in Hampshire County. Northampton is larger than Greenfield, with a population of about 28,000, and its downtown is the cultural hub of the Pioneer Valley. Originally a farming community, Northampton grew into a significant commercial and industrial center, like Greenfield, in the nineteenth century. During the twentieth century, it, too, declined, but it experienced a dramatic revival during the 1980s, when several visionary developers began to restore the historic commercial buildings along Main Street, attracting a lively collection of restaurants, bakeries, boutiques, and art galleries. Adding to the city's vibrant culture are several distinctive performance venues, including the venerable Academy of Music (1891) on Main Street and the Calvin Theater (1924) on King Street (named after Northampton native and US president Calvin Coolidge).

Northampton boasts many buildings of architectural significance, spanning several centuries and various styles. Numerous eighteenth-century houses remain, concentrated primarily on Bridge Street, South Street, and Elm Street. The Historic Northampton museum maintains three restored houses at its Bridge Street campus. Main Street is lined by three- and four-story nineteenth-century commercial buildings, as well as several distinctive civic and religious structures. Many of these are the work of the versatile and prolific local architect William Fenno Pratt, whose most prominent commissions include the quaintly castle-inspired City Hall (210 Main Street, 1849), the Connecticut River Railroad Depot (Strong Avenue, 1865), the Renaissance Revival Smith Charities Building (51 Main Street, 1865), and the Italianate Northampton National Bank (135 Main Street, 1866).

Other Victorian civic buildings of note include two excellent examples of the Richardsonian Romanesque style: the Hampshire County Courthouse by Henry F. Kilbourn (at the corner of Main and King Streets, 1886) and the Forbes Library by William Brocklesby (20 West Street, 1894). Of the several Gothic Revival churches in Northampton, the two most impressive are St. Mary's Catholic Church by Patrick Ford (3 Elm Street, 1881–1895) and the combined First Churches (129 Main Street, 1877), designed by Peabody & Stearns at the same time they were designing the Dickinson High School Building in Deerfield.

Significant twentieth-century landmarks include two buildings on King Street near its intersection with Main Street. The first is the Hotel Northampton, a large Colonial Revival structure designed by H. L. Stevens in 1927. The second is the former First National Bank of Northampton (now Silverscape Designs), a 1928 art deco building by J. Williams Beal, notable for its exquisite interior.

Northampton is also home to Smith College, the prestigious women's school founded in 1871. Smith's beautifully landscaped campus has many notable buildings dating from the Victorian period to the present, and it is the subject of *Smith College: The Campus Guide*, by Margaret B. Vickery (Princeton Architectural Press, 2007). Smith's campus extends west from the center of town along both sides of Elm Street, a neighborhood that also includes an excellent collection of nineteenth-century houses.

The town of Amherst lies just a few miles to the east of Northampton, on the other side of the Connecticut River. Its town center is slightly smaller than that of Northampton, but it has a similar ambiance and architectural character, composed mainly of nineteenth-century civic and commercial buildings. The most notable of

Main Street, Northampton, Massachusetts

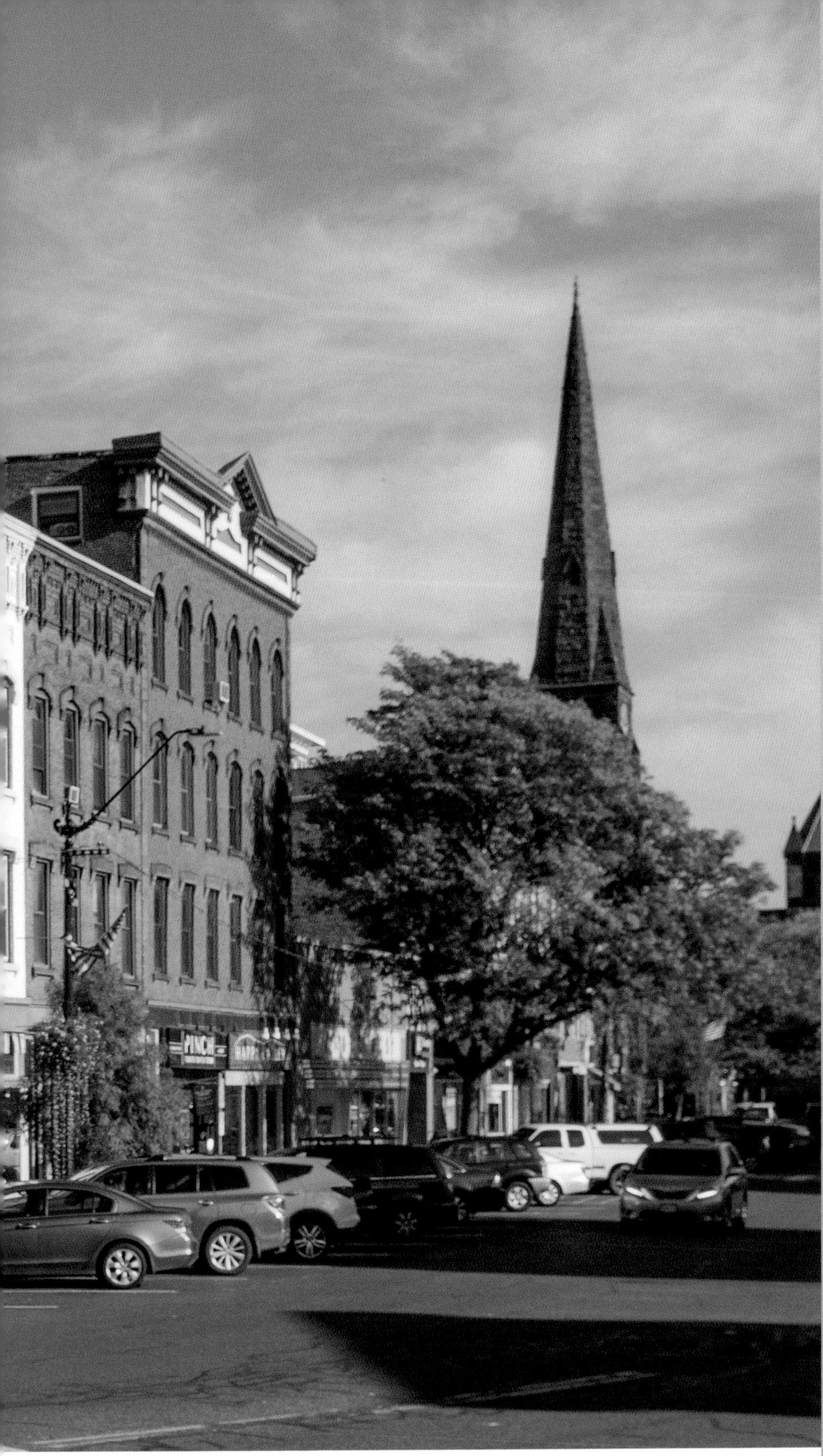
PINCH

First Churches and Hampshire County Courthouse, Northampton , Massachusetts

Grace Episcopal Church (center) and rectory (left); Inn on Boltwood (formerly the Lord Jeffery Inn) (right), Amherst, Massachusetts

these are the 1890 Romanesque Revival Town Hall by H. S. McKay and the 1866 Gothic Revival Grace Episcopal Church by Henry Dudley, both on Boltwood Avenue. Several twentieth-century Colonial Revival buildings can also be found in the town center, including two superb examples by the Boston firm of Putnam & Cox: the Lord Jeffery Inn, which was recently renamed the Inn on Boltwood (30 Boltwood Avenue, 1926) and Jones Library (Amity Street, 1928).

Amherst's downtown is arranged around three sides of a large common. The fourth side opens southward toward the campus of Amherst College, founded in 1821 and today one of the country's leading liberal arts colleges. The alma mater of Deerfield headmaster Frank Boyden, Amherst for many years in the early twentieth century enrolled more Deerfield Academy graduates than any other college or university. (The second most popular destination was Amherst's traditional rival, Williams College.) Conversely, many Deerfield faculty members over the past century were Amherst alumni, and the college's third president was a former Deerfield Academy preceptor, Edward Hitchcock. (See Walk Four, page 155.) Amherst is featured in *Amherst College: The Campus Guide*, by Blair Kamin (Princeton Architectural Press, 2020).

Emily Dickinson House, Amherst , Massachusetts

To the north, somewhat removed from the town center, is the flagship campus of the University of Massachusetts, whose thirty thousand students effectively double the population of the town during the academic year. Founded in 1863 as the Massachusetts Agricultural College, the university expanded dramatically during the second half of the twentieth century. Its campus features a large volume of modernist architecture, including several high-rises that tower incongruously above the surrounding farmland. UMass-Amherst is featured in the *University of Massachusetts Amherst: The Campus Guide*, by Marla R. Miller and Max Page (Princeton Architectural Press, 2013).

The town of Amherst has several neighborhoods lined with significant houses, including the blocks just west of the town center lying to either side of Amity Street. Traveling in the opposite direction, eastward along Main Street, one encounters a series of magnificent nineteenth-century houses on generous lots. Foremost among these is the home of Emily Dickinson, which has been preserved and is open to the public as a museum. This large Greek Revival house is perhaps the finest in Amherst, and its architecture seems to find its way into Dickinson's work, even becoming a metaphor for poetry itself. She wrote:

> I dwell in Possibility —
> A fairer House than Prose —
> More numerous of Windows —
> Superior — for Doors —
>
> Of Chambers as the Cedars —
> Impregnable of eye —
> And for an everlasting Roof
> The Gambrels of the Sky —
>
> Of Visitors — the fairest —
> For Occupation — This —
> The spreading wide my narrow Hands
> To gather Paradise

Boyden Library staircase

Acknowledgments

Many people assisted me in writing this guide, and I am deeply grateful to all of them.

The success of an architectural guide depends on images as much as text, and I was privileged to be able to collaborate on this book with two fellow architects: photographer Robert Barnett and map art director George Knight. In addition to providing compelling illustrations, both lent their expertise by reading and commenting on drafts of the manuscript. To bring the map to life, George worked with the exceptionally talented cartographers Constance Brown and Duncan Milne, of Redstone Studios.

I am indebted to Jan Hartman, the Campus Guide series director at Princeton Architectural Press, who has been endlessly helpful and patient in coordinating all of our efforts and guiding the book from the earliest stages. I would also like to thank the book's editor, Linda Lee, copy editor Laura Didyk, and designer Natalie Snodgrass.

Deerfield Academy has energetically participated in this project from the outset. I am particularly grateful to the former head of school, Margarita O'Byrne Curtis, for her enthusiastic support, without which the book never would have gotten off the ground. Jessica Day, David Thiel, and Cara Cusson of the Academy's Communications Office devoted an enormous amount of time and energy to shaping the guide and ensuring that it would reflect not only Deerfield's distinguished history but also its ambitious and dynamic vision for the future. Anne Lozier, head of the Deerfield Academy Archives, aided my research with her unmatched knowledge of the school's history and provided many of the beautiful archival photos and drawings that supplement Robert Barnett's contemporary photography.

Julia Elliott made countless improvements to the text, in both style and substance, especially by contributing significant biographical information on a number of the people who appear in the narrative.

In addition, many former and current Deerfield Academy faculty members read and commented on early drafts, ensuring accuracy and enriching the narrative with firsthand knowledge of the school's history and architecture. I am particularly grateful to Robert Moorhead, David Howell, Eric Widmer, and David Payne for answering numerous questions and providing insightful feedback on drafts. Chuck Williams and Jeff Galli at the Academy's physical plant also contributed valuable knowledge.

I would like to give special thanks to Robert Moorhead, an inspiring teacher and mentor, who taught the first architectural design courses I ever took (almost two decades ago now) and set me on the path to becoming an architect. I am doubly grateful to him for suggesting that I write this guide and for providing frequent advice along the way.

I would like also to thank Bill Flynt, Historic Deerfield's architectural conservator, who reviewed and commented on several chapters, contributing his vast knowledge of Deerfield's historic houses. Many others at Historic Deerfield assisted with the book, including Philip Zea, David Bosse, Amanda Lange, Christine Ritok, David Lazaro, Daniel Sousa, and Penny Leveritt.

Thanks also to Timothy Neumann, Suzanne Flynt, and Sheila Damkoehler, of the Pocumtuck Valley Memorial Association; Meg Clark and Kim Loughlin, of the Bement School; and Michele Clark, at the Frederick Law Olmsted National Historic Site.

Finally, I am grateful for the support and assistance of my wife, Stavroula Hatzios, who sacrificed many hours she could have spent on her own research in order to read my early drafts and provide her invaluable feedback.

View of Deerfield from Pocumtuck Ridge

Aedicule: A classical architectural frame around a door, window, or niche, consisting of columns or pilasters supporting an entablature.

Arcade: A row of arches.

Arch: A spanning structure, originally in masonry construction, composed of a series of wedge-shaped bricks or stones (voussoirs) held together by compression from the weight of the wall above. Depending on the style of the building, arches may be round, segmental (curved, but not a full half-circle), flat, or pointed.

Architrave: The lowermost of three horizontal elements (along with the frieze and cornice) constitutin a classical entablature. The architrave represents a beam that spans from one column to another.

Art Deco: An abstracted classical style popular during the 1930s and '40s, characterized by geometric forms, blocky massing, and shallow ornamental carving.

Axis: An imaginary straight line describing the center of a bilaterally symmetrical composition.

Balustrade: An ornamental parapet composed of a railing supported by a series of balusters (short, bulging colonnettes), often placed above a cornice.

Baroque: A style of classicism popular in Europe during the seventeenth and eighteenth centuries, characterized by extravagantly curved and interlocking geometries, a profusion of carved ornament, and a sense of spatial drama.

Basilica: An ancient Roman building type subsequently adapted to Christian churches, featuring a large, central space flanked by lower side aisles, which are set apart by colonnades or arcades. The difference in height between the main volume and the side aisles often allows for a row of windows above the roof of the side aisle, admitting light into the central space. This is known as a *clerestory*.

Bay Window: A window that is curved or polygonal in plan, such that it projects outward from a wall.

Beaux-Arts: A style of classicism taught at the École des Beaux-Arts in Paris, the most prestigious architecture school during the nineteenth century. This mode of design, which was especially employed for monumental civic buildings, emphasizes symmetry, rational planning, and the enrichment of architecture with sculpture, painting, and other decorative arts.

Bond: One of several standard patterns for laying bricks to build a wall. Bricks laid with their long side visible are called stretchers; those laid with the short side visible are called headers. Some frequently seen bonds include common bond (all stretchers, except for every fifth or sixth row, which is composed of headers), English bond (rows of stretchers alternate with rows of headers), and Flemish bond (stretchers and headers alternate within each row).

Capital: The uppermost part of a classical column, composed of moldings and carved elements arranged to create an artful transition between the cylindrical geometry of a column shaft and the rectangular geometry of the beam (entablature) above.

Carolean: Belonging to the period in England during the reign of King Charles II, during the second half of the seventeenth century. See also *Georgian*.

Casement Window: A type of window in which the sash is hinged on one side so that it can open by swinging horizontally outward. See also *double-hung window*.

Classical Architecture: Developed in ancient Greece and Rome, and revived throughout Europe during the Renaissance, classicism is the foundation for most subsequent stylistic developments in the history of Western architecture. It is based on the stylized representation of a post-and-beam structural system and governed by one of several proportional and compositional systems known as orders.

Colonial Revival: A style originating in the 1870s and reaching its peak in the 1920s and 1930s, which found inspiration in the eighteenth-century architecture of colonial America. See also *Queen Anne*.

Column: A post or vertical structural member. In classical architecture, a column comprises three parts, the base, shaft, and capital, and it supports a horizontal beam or entablature.

Colonnade: A row of columns and their entablature.

Composite: One of the classical orders originating in ancient Rome. It is characterized by slender proportions and recognizable by its column capitals, which combine the scrolls (volutes) of the Ionic with the acanthus leaves of the Corinthian.

Corinthian: One of the classical orders originating in ancient Greece. It is characterized by slender proportions and recognizable by its highly ornate column capitals of carved acanthus leaves.

Cornice: The classical treatment of an eave. The uppermost part of a classical entablature, consisting of a series of moldings that step progressively outward from the face of the wall or column.

Cupola: A small decorative structure sitting on top of a roof. Often, it includes windows to illuminate the space below.

Doric: One of the classical orders, originating in ancient Greece. It features stout proportions and simple details.

Dormer: A structure that projects from a sloped roof to allow for a window.

Double-Hung Window: A type of window consisting of two sashes that open by sliding vertically past one another. Invented in the late seventeenth century and used extensively in the Netherlands, England, and the United States from the eighteenth century onward. Sashes often consist of multiple smaller panes of glass, held in place by wood muntins. See also *casement window*.

Eave: That part of a pitched roof that overhangs the face of the wall below.

Ell: An addition to the rear of a house, typically with the ridge perpendicular to the house's main facade.

Entablature: In classical architecture, the series of horizontal elements that span from one column to another. The entablature comprises, from bottom to top, the architrave, frieze, and cornice.

Facade: The face of a building.

Federal: A style popular in the United States from about 1790 to 1830. A delicate classicism inspired by ancient Roman wall paintings, often employing attenuated proportions and elliptical profiles.

Flutes: Vertical channels carved into the surface of a column or pilaster. Classical columns may be either fluted or unfluted.

Frieze: The middle of three horizontal elements constituting a classical entablature. It sits between the architrave below and the cornice above. Unlike the other two parts of the entablature, the frieze is a flat plane, though it is sometimes ornamented with carved inscriptions or sculpture.

Frontispiece: A central, projecting portion of a facade, often more elaborate than the rest of the building.

Gable: The triangular portion of a wall that sits between the two sides of a sloped roof.

Gambrel Roof: A roof having two pitches, a steeper plane below and a shallower one above. This type of roof construction creates more usable space within.

Georgian: The style of architecture popular in England and its colonies in the eighteenth century (during the reigns of the Hanoverian kings George I, II, and III). The style arises from classicism of the Renaissance and Baroque. See also *Carolean*.

Gothic: A style developed in France in the twelfth century and used throughout Europe during the subsequent four centuries, characterized by an emphasis on verticality. Pointed arches are the most readily identifiable hallmark of this style. Gothic architecture is often thought of in contrast to classicism, though certain compositional similarities may be observed.

Gothic Revival: A revival of the Gothic style originating in England during the eighteenth century and first appearing in the United States in the early nineteenth century. It remained popular, especially for churches, until the early twentieth century.

Greek Revival: A revival of Greek classical architecture highly popular in the United States between the 1820s and the 1840s.

Hipped Roof: A roof that is pitched on all four sides.

Ionic: One of the classical orders originating in ancient Greece. It can be recognized by its column capitals, which are composed of scrolled volutes.

Italianate: A style of architecture popular in the United States during the 1850s and 1860s, inspired by the villas of central Italy. The most common hallmark of this style is a very low pitched roof with deeply projecting eaves.

Lintel: A beam (most often of stone) spanning an opening in a masonry wall.

Masonry: A type of construction using stone and/or brick, typically held together with mortar.

Modernism: An architectural style developed in Europe in the early twentieth century and popularized in the United States after World War II. It was founded on a revolutionary rejection of all previous architectural styles and celebrated the visual characteristics of industrial machinery and mass production. It was also known as the International Style because it was intended to be universally applicable and not influenced by local or national architectural traditions.

Muntins: The thin vertical and horizontal members (typically wood) that hold the panes of glass within a window sash.

Order: One of several standardized proportional and compositional systems governing classical architecture. Each order consists of a column, the pedestal it sits on, and the entablature it supports. The most common orders, developed in Greco-Roman antiquity and revived by architects of the Renaissance, are the Tuscan, Doric, Ionic, Corinthian, and Composite.

Palladian: The style inspired by the work of the Renaissance architect Andrea Palladio (1508–1580), who worked in and around Venice in the sixteenth century and became broadly influential, especially in England and the United States, by means of his popular illustrated treatise *I Quattro Libri dell'Architettura* ("The Four Books of Architecture"). His villa designs are marked by a strong bilateral symmetry and often feature a classical portico at the center.

Pedestal: In classical architecture, a block that supports a column, raising it off the ground. Pedestals typically have moldings at their base and top.

Pediment: A classical gable. The triangular region of a facade formed by angled cornices (following the pitched planes of the roof) and the horizontal line of the entablature below. The roof pitches are usually low and are sometimes replaced with a segment of a circle or scrolled S-curves (ogees). When the apex is omitted, it is known as a broken pediment.

Picturesque: A romantic compositional strategy, applied to both architecture and landscape design that rejects highly ordered geometries, especially bilateral symmetry, in order to appear naturalistic or unplanned.

Pier: A freestanding square post, often supporting an arch rather than a beam.

Pilaster: The architectural representation of a column embedded in a wall. It follows the same proportions and details of a column but is rectangular in plan rather than circular.

Pitched Roof: A roof that is sloped to shed water in two directions with a ridge down the middle.

Plinth: A block or platform serving as the base for an architectural element or an entire building.

Portico: A classical porch, like those that characterized the facades of Roman temples. Usually composed of columns supporting an entablature with a pediment.

Postmodernism: A style popular in the United States between the 1970s and the 1990s, developed in reaction to the austerity of modernism. It reintroduced to architecture the idea of historical allusion, though it typically did so in a highly simplified, ironic, even comical manner.

Queen Anne: A delicate and whimsical style of architecture popular in England and the United States between the 1870s and the 1890s. It took inspiration from seventeenth-century English architecture. See also *Colonial Revival*.

Quoins: Large rectangular stones (or the architectural representation thereof) that structurally and/or visually reinforce the corners of a building.

Renaissance Revival: A style of architecture popular in the United States in the late nineteenth century that was based on the urban architecture of the Italian Renaissance.

Richardsonian Romanesque: A style of architecture invented by the American architect Henry Hobson Richardson (1838–1886) and widely emulated in the years following his death. It was inspired by the medieval architecture of southern France prior to the development of the Gothic. The style is heavy yet picturesque and features round arches and polychrome masonry.

Rustication: The carving of masonry so as to emphasize the individual stones, recessing the mortar joints. Often the surface of the stones is made rough or textured, in contrast with the smooth surface of ashlar masonry.

String Course: A horizontal band of masonry that projects slightly from the face of a wall.

Transom Window: A horizontal window running just above a door.

Tuscan: One of the classical orders, originating in ancient Rome. It is the stoutest and simplest of the orders.

Victorian: The historical period defined by the reign of Queen Victoria (1837–1901). This period was characterized by quickly changing architectural fashions in England and the United States, often marked by eclecticism and the adoption of exotic and/or historical styles valued for their romantic associations. Styles during this period included the Italianate, Egyptian Revival, Gothic Revival, Romanesque Revival, and Renaissance Revival, among others.

Volutes: The carved scrolls found in the column capitals of the Ionic and Composite orders.

Voussoirs: The wedge-shaped bricks or stones constituting an arch. The central voussoir of an arch is often visually emphasized and is known as the keystone.

John Louis Dormitory

Bibliography

REPOSITORIES

Avery Library, Columbia University
Deerfield Academy Archives
Memorial Libraries of the Pocumtuck Valley Memorial Association and Historic Deerfield

PERIODICALS

Deerfield Magazine
The Deerfield Scroll
The New York Times

PUBLICATIONS

Chamberlain, Samuel, and Henry Flynt. *Frontier of Freedom: The Portrait of an Extraordinary Village, Old Deerfield, Massachusetts*. New York: Hastings House, 1952.

Coleman, Emma Lewis. *A Historic and Present Day Guide to Old Deerfield*. Boston: [s.n.], 1907.

Flynt, Suzanne L. *Gathered and Preserved*. Deerfield, MA: Pocumtuck Valley Memorial Association, 1991.

Fraker, G. Alan, Karinne T. Heise, and Thomas A. Heise. *The Deerfield Reader*. New York: American Heritage, 1996.

Garvin, James L. *A Building History of Northern New England*. Hanover, NH: University Press of New England, 2001.

Herbert, Robert L., and Daria d'Arienzo. *Orra White Hitchcock: An Amherst Woman of Art and Science*. Amherst, MA: Meade Art Museum, Amherst College, 2011.

Hitchcock, Edward. *Reminiscences of Amherst College*. Northampton, MA: Bridgeman & Childs, 1863.

———. *Report on the Geology, Mineralogy, Botany, and Zoology of Massachusetts*. Amherst,MA: Press of J. S. and C. Adams, 1833.

Lee, Nancy M. *Samuel Willard: Minister, Educator, Musician, Agent of Change*. Deerfield, MA: Pocumtuck Valley Memorial Association, 2006.

Marr, Harriet Webster. *The Old New England Academies*. New York: Comet Press Book, 1959.

McAlester, Virginia Savage. *A Field Guide to American Houses*. New York: Knopf, 2013.

McGowan, Susan, and Amelia F. Miller. *Family & Landscape: Deerfield Homelots from 1671*. Deerfield, MA: Pocumtuck Valley Memorial Association, 1996.

McLachlan, James. *American Boarding Schools: A Historical Study*. New York: Scribner, 1970.

McPhee, John. *The Headmaster*. New York: Farrar, Straus and Giroux, 1966.

Melvoin, Richard I. *New England Outpost: War and Society in Colonial Deerfield*. New York: Norton, 1989.

Miller, Peter S., and Kyle J. Scott. *Images of America: Deerfield*. Charleston, SC: Arcadia Press, 2002.

Moorhead, Andrea. *The Hearth: A Deerfield Academy Tradition*. Deerfield, MA: Deerfield Academy Press, 2003.

Moorhead, Robert, and Andrea Moorhead. *Deerfield 1797–1997: A Pictorial History of the Academy*. Deerfield, MA: Deerfield Academy Press, 1997.

Morgan, Keith N. *Charles A. Platt: The Artist as Architect*. New York and Cambridge: Architectural History Foundation and MIT Press, 1985.
———. *Shaping an American Landscape: The Art and Architecture of Charles A. Platt*. Hanover, NH: University Press of New England, 1995.
Morrison, Hugh. *Early American Architecture, from the First Colonial Settlements to the National Period*. New York: Dover, 1987.
Palladio, Andrea. *The Four Books on Architecture*. Cambridge: MIT Press, 2001.
Robinson, Annie. *Peabody & Stearns: Country Houses and Seaside Cottages*. New York: Norton, 2010.
Sheldon, George, ed. *Catalogue of the Collection of Relics in Memorial Hall, Deerfield, Mass., U.S.A., Gathered and Preserved by the Pocumtuck Valley Memorial Association*. Deerfield, MA: PVMA, 1908.
———. *A History of Deerfield Massachusetts*. Deerfield, MA: Pocumtuck Valley Memorial Association, 2004.
———, ed. *History and Proceedings of the Pocumtuck Valley Memorial Association*. Deerfield,MA: PVMA, 1890.
———. *Joseph Stebbins: A Pioneer at the Outbreak of the Revolution*. Salem. MA: Salem Press Company, 1916.
Sheldon, Jennie Maria Arms. *Charlotte Alice Baker: A Tribute*. Greenfield, MA: Recorder Press, 1910.
———. *The Evolutionary History of a New England Homestead: The Colonial Joseph Stebbins Homestead in Deerfield, Massachusetts*. Brattleboro, VT: E.L. Hildreth, 1925.
Stillinger, Elizabeth. *Historic Deerfield: A Portrait of Early America*. New York: Dutton Studio Books, 1992.
Widmer, Eric, ed. *Deerfield Remembers: A Festschrift for Frank Learoyd Boyden, 1902–2002*. Deerfield,MA: Deerfield Academy Press, 2004.
Wilson, Richard Guy. *The Colonial Revival House*. New York: Harry N. Abrams, 2004.

Image Credits

All photographs are by Robert S. Barnett unless otherwise noted.

Deerfield Academy Archives: 35, 58, 73, 74, 87b, 93, 112, 113, 119, 129, 157
Jim Gipe, 2005: 70
Jim Gipe, 2006: 148
Aaron M. Helfand: 14, 23, 76, 84, 111, 153, 154, 173l, 178, 196, 197, 198, 204, 214
Henry N. Flynt Library, Historic Deerfield: 16
Historic Deerfield: 182
National Park Service, Frederick Law Olmsted National Historic Site: 37
Pocumtuck Valley Memorial Association's Memorial Hall Museum: 15, 18

Main School Building, Arms Building, and Pocumtuck buttonball tree

Page references for illustrations appear in *italics*.

Academy Building, 26, 27–29, 33, 40, 162
See also Memorial Hall Museum (Benjamin)
Academy of Music, Northampton, 193
Adams, Samuel, 20
Addison Gallery, Phillips Academy (Platt), 40
Allen, Frances and Mary, *18–19*, 159
Allen House, 139, *145*, 152, 159–61, *160*, 164, 183
American Architect and Building News, 34–35
American elm trees, *65*, 83–86, *84–85*
American Revolution, 154
Amherst, Massachusetts, 168, 191, 193, *197*, 197–99, *198*
Amherst College, 156, 197
Amherst College: The Campus Guide **(Kamin),** 197
Andrewes, William, 55–56, *57*
Architects' Collaborative, 188
Architectural Components, 111
Architectural Resources Cambridge (ARC), 55, 67, 69, 72, 75, 99, 100–101, *101*, 139–43, *140–41*, *142–43*
Arms, George Albert, 43, 46, 183, 187
Arms Building (Platt), 25, 43–48, *44–45*, *47*, *48*, 49, 50, 56, 68, 72, 73, 75, 93, 132, 162, 168
Asa Stebbins House, *13*, 75
Ashley, Jonathan, 120, 146, 162–63
Ashley, Tom, 109–10
Ashley House, *119*, 120, 142, *145*, 159, 162–64, *164*, *165*, 183
Athletic Center, 13, *65*, 66, 88–100, *90–91*, *92*, *93*, *94*, *95*, *96–97*, *98–99*, *100*
Atkin, Tony, 69, *70–71*, 72, 78, 82
Atkin Olshin Schade Architects, 67, 69
Audubon, John James, 69
Austin, John P. N., 26, 152

Bailey, Lynn Gordon Jr., 86
Baker, C. Alice, 146, 169, 173, 182–83
Bank Row, Greenfield, 192, *192*
Bardwell, Thomas, 159
Barn, The, *74*, 74–75, 132
Barnard, Joseph, 149, 169
Barnard, Salah, 181
Barton, Bruce, 12, 124–25
Barton Dormitory (William & Geoffrey Platt), *103*, *124*, 124–25
Barton House, 190
Battle of Belleau Wood, 110
Bauhaus, 55
Beal, J. Williams, 193
Bement, Grace and Lewis, 189–90
Bement House, 189
Bement School, *167*, 168, 189–91, *190*
Benjamin, Asher, *27*, 27–33, *28*, *30*, *31*, *32*, 74, 162, 174, 192
Bewkes House, *102*, 115, *116–17*, 118, 120, 121, 187
Birds of America **(Audubon),** 69
Boston Society of Natural History, 72
Boston Tea Party, 152, 154
Boyden, Frank L., 20, 26, 36–37, 40, 41, 42, 50, 56, 66, 73, 78, 86, 92–93, 101, 105, 109, 110, 112–14, 124, 125, 146, 148, 152, 158, 159, 187, 197
Boyden Hall (Drew), 41, *112*, 112–13, 114, 121, 139
Boyden, Helen Childs, 26, 42, 50, 56, 114, 146, 148, 152
Boyden Library. *See* Frank L. and Helen Childs Boyden Library (William & Geoffrey Platt)
Brick Church (Clapp), 36, 49, 118, 149, 152, *167*, 168, 175, *176–77*, *178*, 178–80, *179*
Brocklesby, William, 193

Brooke's Garden, 25, 50, *51*
Brown, Howard Howland, 88
Bulfinch, Charles, 28
Bull, John Partridge, 146
Butterfield, Richard, 28

Calvin Theater, Northampton, 193
Caswell Library, 42, *42*, 46, 55
Center for Service and Global Citizenship, 12
Chapin Dormitory, 118
Cheney, Frank, 30
Childs, David, *11*, *25*, 58–63, *60–61*, *62*, 86, 94, *94*, *95*, 98, *100*, *134–35*, *136*, 136–39, *137*, *138*, *211*
Choragic Monument of Thrasyllus, 74
cider stone, *89*
City Hall, Northampton (Pratt), 193
Civil War Memorial, 169
Clapp, Winthrop, 36, 49, 118, 149, 152, 168, 175, *176–77*, *178*, 178–80, *179*
Class of 1953 Gymnasium (Platt), *8*, 46, 49, 68, 75, *93*, 93–94
Class of 1993 Hockey Rink (William & Geoffrey Platt, Sasaki Associates), 94, *98–99*, 99
Cochran, Thomas, 37, 40
Cochran Chapel, Phillips Academy (Platt), 40
Coleman-Hollister House, Greenfield (Benjamin), 192
College Hall, Smith College (Peabody & Stearns), 34
Colonial Revival style, *35*, 35–36, *38–39*, 40, *41*, *42*, *66*, *93*, *112*, *113*, *121*, *122*, *123*, *124*, *142–43*, *186*
Colonial Williamsburg, 37
Connecticut River, 15, 42, 101, 156, 162, 168, 191, 193
Connecticut River Conservancy, 192
Connecticut River Railroad Depot, Northampton (Pratt), 193
Coolidge, Calvin, 193
Cooper, Frank Irving, 41, 50, 68, 72, 113, *113*, 114, 121, 125, 132, 148–49
Cottonwood tree, *103*, *111*, 111–12
***Country Almanac* (Hitchcock),** 156
Cram and Ferguson, 75
Crow, Robert, 128
Crow Commons, 128
Curtis, Margarita O'Byrne, 26, 142, 152

Damon, Isaac, 179
David H. Koch Field House (Sasaki Associates), 99–100, *100*
Deerfield, Massachusetts
history, 15–22
map, *16*
***Deerfield Academy* (Barton),** 12
***Deerfield Collection of Sacred Music* (Willard),** 149
Deerfield Historical Commission, 169
Deerfield Inn, 159, *167*, 183, *186*, 187
Deerfield Medal, 125
Deerfield River, 12, 15, 17, *17*, *21*, 59, 86, 100–101
Deerfield Society of Arts and Crafts, 152
DeNunzio, Ralph and Jean, 129
DeNunzio Dormitory (Edward Larrabee Barnes Associates), 75, *103*, 129, *129*, 132, *133*, 138
Dewey Dormitory and Health Center (William & Geoffrey Platt), *65*, 66, 75–78, *76–77*, *130*, 132, *133*
Dewey Squash Courts, 99, *100*
Dickinson, Consider "Uncle Sid," 33–34
Dickinson, Emily, *198*, 199
Dickinson, Esther, 33–34
Dickinson High School (Peabody & Stearns), 33–36, *35*, 105, 110, 112, 137–38, 193
Dining Hall (William & Geoffrey Platt), *8*, 49, *65*, 66, 78–83, *79*, *80–81*, *82–83*, 113, 132, 158

Dormitory Quadrangles, *102–3*, 125–39, *126*, *127*, *128*, *129*, *130*, *131*, *133*, *134–35*, *136*, *137*, *138*
Douglas, Thomas, 82
Drew, M. R., 41, *112*, 112–13, 114, 121, 139
Dudley, Governor Joseph (Massachusetts), 172
Dudley, Henry, 197
Duffy, Roger, 58–63, *60–61*, *62*, 86, 98, 136
Dwight House, 183

Eaglebrook School, *166*, 168, 187–88, *188–89*, 191
East Gym (Platt), *90–91*, *93*
Edward Larrabee Barnes Associates, 75, 129, *129*, 132, *133*, 137, 138
Elizabeth Wachsman Concert Hall, 72
Emily Dickinson House, Amherst, *198*, 199
Ensign John Sheldon House, 29–30, *32*, 35
See also Old Indian House
Ephraim Williams House, 114, *144*, 146–49, *147*, *148*, 155
Everett House, 187

Family & Landscape: Deerfield Homelots from 1671 **(McGowan, Miller),** 22
Field Dormitory (William & Geoffrey Platt), *103*, 120, 125, *127*
First Churches, Northampton (Peabody & Stearns), 193, *196*
First Congregational Church. *See* Brick Church
First National Bank of Northampton, Northampton (Beal), 193
First National Bank & Trust Company, Greenfield, 192
Flynt, Henry and Helen, 22, 75, 120, 146, 152, 159–61, 164, 178, 183, 187
Flynt, William, 160
Flynt Center for Early American Life, 111
Forbes Library, Northampton (Brocklesby), 193
Ford, Patrick, 193
Frank L. and Helen Childs Boyden Library (William & Geoffrey Platt), 12, *25*, 50–55, *52–53*, *54*, 56, 67, *200–201*
Franklin County Courthouse, Greenfield, 192
Franklin Savings Bank, Greenfield, 192
Frary, Nathaniel, 181
Frary House and Barnard Tavern, 20, *166*, 173, *181*, 181–83, *182*, 183
French and Indian raids, 16, 29, 30, 110, 146, 161, 168, 169, 172–73, 174, 182
French and Indian Wars, 146, 172, 173
Fuller, Arthur, 159
Fuller, George, 158–59

Gass, William, 146, 161, 164, *174*, 174–75, 183
Georgian/Colonial Revival style, *44–45*, *47*, *48*, *49*, *150–51*
Gibbs, Howard, 187
Girls Club, 72–74, *73*, 162
Glee Club, 75
Gonzalez, Brooke, 50
Gordie Center for Substance Abuse Prevention, University of Virginia, 86
Gordie's Overlook, 86, *87*
Gothic Revival style, *197*
Grace Episcopal Church, Amherst (Dudley), 197, *197*
Greek Revival style, *73*, 73–74, *180*, *198*
Greek War of Independence, 74
Greenfield, Massachusetts, 168, 191–92, *192*
Greenfield Gazette and Courier, 35
Greenfield Public Library, Greenfield, 192
See also Leavitt-Hovey House, Greenfield (Benjamin)
Greer Store, *92*, 93
Gropius, Walter, 55, 59

Gymnasium. *See* Class of 1953 Gymnasium (Platt)

Haas House, 191
Hall Tavern, *167*, 183, *184–85*
Hammerschlag Boathouse (Architectural Resources Cambridge), *65*, 100–101, *101*
Hampshire County Courthouse, Northampton (Kilbourn), 193, *196*
Hampson, J. R., 75
Harold Webster Smith Dormitory (Architectural Resources Cambridge), 75, *103*, 139, *140–41*, 143
Haynes House, *102*, *115*, 118, 120, 121
***Headmaster, The* (McPhee),** 41
Headmaster's Field, *65*, 86–88, *88–89*
Helen Childs Boyden Science Center (Ward), *25*, 56–58, *58*, 63, 72
Henry Varnum Poor, *68*
***Herbarium Parvum Pictum* (Hitchcock),** 156, *157*
Heritage Foundation. *See* Historic Deerfield
Herrick, Claudius, 27
Hess Center for the Arts, 12, 13, 27, 50, *65*, 66, *66*, 67–72, *68*, *70–71*, 88
Hildreth, Hosea, 149
Hilson Art Gallery (William & Geoffrey Platt), 69, 72
Hinsdale and Anna Williams House, *104–5*
Historic Deerfield, 22, 33, 146, 159–60, 161, 162, 164, 168, 181, 183, 187
***Historic Deerfield: A Portrait of Early America* (Stillinger),** 22
Historic Northampton, 193
***History of Deerfield, Massachusetts, A* (Sheldon),** 162, 163, 178
"History of Memorial Hall" (Sheldon), 30
Hitchcock, Edward and Orra White, 15, 22, 155–56, *157*, 197
Hitchcock, Justin, 155
Hitchcock, Nathaniel, 178
Hitchcock House, *6–7*, 78, 139, *144*, *155*, 155–58, 159
Hodermarsky, Daniel, 68
Hotel Northampton (Stevens), 193
Hoyt, Arthur, 115, 118
Hoyt, Epaphras and Experience, 115
Huffard, Wick, 86, 88
Huffard Garden, 86
Hyatt, Alpheus, 72

Infirmary, 49
Inn on Boltwood, Amherst (Putnam & Cox), 197, *197*
Italianate style, *115*, *116–17*, *119*

John Louis Dormitory (Childs), *11*, *102*, *134–35*, 136, *136*, 137, 138, *211*
John Russell Cutlery Company, 189
Johnson-Doubleday Dormitory (Timothy Smith & Associates), 56, *103*, *128*, 128–29, 132, 138
John Williams House, 50, *103*, *106–7*, *108*, 109–11, *111*, 112, 125, 139, 146, 148, 155, 159, 162, 178
Jones, Margot, 190, 191
Jones Library, Amherst (Putnam & Cox), 197
Jones Whitsett Architects, 190
Joseph Stebbins House, 121, *145*, 152, *154*, 154–55

Kamin, Blair, 197
Kaufmann, Robert, 26, 152
Kendall Classroom Building (William & Geoffrey Platt), *25*, 48–50, *49*, 175

Kilbourn, Henry F., 193, *196*
King William's War, 168
Kirkham & Parlett, 158
Koch, David, 59
Koch Center for Science, Mathematics and Technology (Childs, Duffy), 13, *25*, 27, 58–63, *60–61*, *62*, 86, 98, 136
Koch Natatorium (Childs), 59, 86, *94*, *95*, *96–97*, 98, *100*, 136
Kravis Arena, 93
Kuhn Riddle Architects, 149, 190

Lane, Susan Minot, 173, 182
Large Auditorium, 67, 69
Latrobe, Benjamin, 46
Laurel Hill Cemetery, 169
Leavitt-Hovey House, Greenfield (Benjamin), 192
LEED (Leadership in Energy and Environmental Design) certification, 63
Lincoln, Luther, 149
Little Brown House, 139, *144*, 152, *158*, 158–59
Longitude Dial (Andrewes), *25*, 55–56, *57*
Lord Jeffery Inn, Amherst. *See* Inn on Boltwood, Amherst (Putnam & Cox)
Louis Marx Dormitory (Childs), *102*, 136, *137*, *138*
Lower Level, 66, 78, 86, *87*, 98, 169

Main School Building (Platt), *25*, 26, 36–42, *38–39*, *41*, *42*, 46, 49, 50, 54, 55, 59, 68, 72, 75, 93, 94, 113, 115, 125, 132, 137, 158, 168
Manse, The, 121, *144*, 148, 149–52, *150–51*, *153*, 154, 155, 158, 159, 168, 182
Massachusetts Agricultural College. *See* University of Massachusetts, Amherst
Mather Dormitory (William & Geoffrey Platt), *103*, 118, 120, *122*, 137
Matthews Hall, Harvard University (Peabody & Stearns), 34
McAlister Dormitory (William & Geoffrey Platt), *103*, 120, *126*
McGowan, Susan, 22
McKay, H. S., 197
McPhee, John, 41
meetinghouses and churches, *166–67*, 175–81, *176–77*, *178*, *179*, *180*
Memorial Building (William & Geoffrey Platt), 49, 50, 54, *66*, 67, 68, 69, 72, 132
See also Hess Center for the Arts
Memorial Hall Museum (Benjamin), *24*, 26, *27*, 27–33, *28*, *30*, *31*, *32*, 162, 174
midcentury Colonial Revival Dormitories, *103*, 120–24, *121*, *122*, *123*, *124*
Mies van der Rohe, 59
Miller, Amelia, 22
Miller, Marla R., 198
modernist style, *58*, *60–61*, *62*

Morsman Tennis Pavilion (Sasaki Associates), 86

Native Americans, 16, 29, 168, 169, 172, 173
New Dorm. *See* O'Byrne Curtis Dormitory (Architectural Resources Cambridge)
Northampton, Massachusetts, 168, 191, 192–93, *194–95*, *196*
Northampton National Bank, Northampton (Pratt), 193

O'Byrne Curtis Dormitory (Architectural Resources Cambridge), *102*, 139, 142–43, *142–43*
Old Burying Ground and 1704 Memorial, 120, *167*, 168, 169–73, *172*, *173*
Old Deerfield Arms Hotel, 113
See also Pocumtuck Dormitory
Old Fort Well, 169

Old Indian House, 115, 149, 161, 174–75
Old Indian House Memorial (Gass), *167*, *174*, 174–75
Old Main Street, *18–19*, 22, *23*, 120, 121, 125, 181, 189
Oliver Wendell Holmes Library, Phillips Academy (Platt), 40
Olmsted Brothers, *37*
One World Trade Center, New York City (Childs), 98
Orthodox Congregational Church. ***See* White Church**

Page, Max, 198
Palladian style, 55, 68, *93*, 94, 125, 132
Palladio, Andrea, 94
Peabody, Robert, 34–35
Peabody & Stearns, 33–36, *35*, 40, 59, 105, 110, 112, 137–38, 193, *196*
Perry, Shaw & Hepburn, 37, 40
Platt, Charles, *8*, 26, 36–42, *38–39*, *41*, *42*, 43–48, *44–45*, *47*, *48*, 49, 50, 54, 55, 56, 59, 68, 72, 73, 75, *90–91*, *93*, 93–94, 113, 115, 120, 125, 132, 137, 158, 162, 168
Plunkett, Charles, 114
Plunkett Dormitory (Cooper), 41, 50, 68, 72, 113, 114, 121, 125, 132, 148
Plunkett Quadrangle, *84–85*
Pocumtuck buttonball tree, *25*, 42, *43*
Pocumtuck Dormitory (William & Geoffrey Platt), *103*, 113, 120, *121*, 181, 187
Pocumtuck Hotel. ***See* Deerfield Inn**
Pocumtuck Ridge, 12, *14*, 15, *15*, 17, 22, 101, 187, *204*
Pocumtuck Valley Memorial Association (PVMA), 20, 28, 29, 30, 31, 33, 162, 173, 175, 183, 191
Polk Building, 190
Poor, Henry Varnum, *68*, 69
Post Office, *177*, 178
Pratt, William Fenno, 193
Pushkin Gallery, Greenfield, 192
Putnam, Annie, 146, 152, 158, 159
Putnam & Cox, 197, *197*
PVMA. *See* Pocumtuck Valley Memorial Association
Pynchon, David, 26, 56

Quabbin Reservoir, 190
Quad, 27, 46, 50, 54, 66, 69, 72, 86, 112, 125, 137, 139
Queen Anne style, 34–35, 192

***Redeemed Captive Returning to Zion, The* (Williams),** 173
Reed, Joseph, 68, 69
Reed Center for the Arts (Atkin), 69, *70–71*, 72, 78
Reid Black Box Theater (Atkin), 69, 72
***Report on the Geology, Mineralogy, Botany, and Zoology of Massachusetts* (Hitchcock),** 15, 156
Richards, Fowkes & Co., 180
Richardson, H. H., 114
Richardsonian Romanesque style, 114
Romano, Giulio, 94
Rosenwald, John and Pat, 129
Rosenwald-Shumway Dormitory (Edward Larrabee Barnes Associates), *103*, 114, 129, *129*, *131*, 132, 137
Russell, William, 162

Sasaki Associates, 86, 94, 99–100, *100*
Scaife Dormitory (William & Geoffrey Platt), *103*, 115, 118, 120, 121, *121*, *123*, 137
Severance, Joseph, 189
Sexton, David, 158
Shaw, Richard Norman, 35
Sheldon, Ensign John, 161, 174

Sheldon, George and Jennie Arms, 30, 31, 33, 43, 72–73, 146, 154, 155, 161–62, 163, 178, 182, 183
Sheldon, John III, 161
Sheldon House, 121, *145*, 154, 161–62, *163*
Shepley, Rutan & Coolidge, 182
Shumway, Forrest and Patsy, 129
Silverscape Designs, 193
Skidmore, Owings & Merrill, *25*, 58–63, *60–61*, *62*, 98, 136
Smith, Harold Webster, 139
Smith, Mr. and Mrs. James C., 139
Smith, Mr. and Mrs. Winthrop Jr., 139
Smith, Mrs. Harold Webster, 139
Smith, Timothy, 56, *128*
Smith Charities Building, Northampton (Pratt), 193
Smith College, 193
***Smith College: The Campus Guide* (Vickery),** 193
Snively House, 189, 190
Stebbins, Joseph Jr., 152, 154, 162
Stevens, H. L., 193
Stillinger, Elizabeth, 22
St. Mary's Catholic Church, Northampton (Ford), 193
Street, The. *See* Old Main Street

Thomas Douglas Architects, 118
Timothy Smith & Associates, 56, *128*, 128–29, 132, 138

Town Common, 24, 26, 29, 36, 46, 49, 93, 110, 146, *167*, 168–69, *170–71*, 175
Town Hall, Amherst (McKay), 197
Trinity Church, Boston (Richardson), 114
***True Stories of New England Captives Carried to Canada during the Old French and Indian Wars* (Baker),** 173

University of Massachusetts, Amherst, 198
***University of Massachusetts Amherst: The Campus Guide* (Miller, Page),** 198
US Capitol Building (Latrobe), 46
US International 420 Sailing Team, 50

Vaudreuil, Governor (New France), 172
Vickery, Margaret B., 193
Von Auersperg Gallery (Architectural Resources Cambridge), 72

Ward, Robertson Jr., *25*, 56–58, *58*, 63
West Gym (William & Geoffrey Platt), 49
White Church, 118, *166*, *180*, 180–81
Widmer, Eric, 26, 152
Willard, Samuel, 30, 146, 149, 161, 174, 179, 180
William & Geoffrey Platt, *8*, 26, 48–50, *49*, 50–55, *52–53*, *54*, 56, 66, *66*, 67, 68, 69, 72, 75–78, *76–77*, 94, *98–99*, 99, 113, 120–24, *121*, *122*, *123*, *124*, 124–25, *127*, *130*, 132, *133*, 137, 158, 175, 181, 187, *200–201*
Williams, Captain Ephraim, 148
Williams, Colonel Ephraim, 146
Williams, Elijah, 34
Williams, Israel, 146
Williams, John, 110, 146, 169, 172–73, *173*
Williams College, 146, 197
Williams Museum, 31
Windigo Architects, 188
Winthrop and Margaret Smith Family Foundation, 139
Wynne, Madeline, 146, 152, 158, 159

Young Ladies Literary Society, 156

Zuber & Cie, 82, *82–83*

Wells-Thorn House, Historic Deerfield

DEERFIELD ACADEMY
BE WORTHY OF YOUR HERITAGE
FOUNDED 1797